NEW EDITION

MARKET LEADER

ELEMENTARY BUSINESS ENGLISH PRACTICE FILE

John Rogers

PEARSON
Longman
www.longman.com

FT
FINANCIAL TIMES

Map of the Practice File

The sounds of English: page 52   **Sounds and spelling**: page 53   **Shadowing**: page 53

	Language work			Talk business	
	Vocabulary	**Language review**	**Writing**	**Sound work**	**Survival business English**
Unit 7 **People** page 28 / page 66	Words for talking about people and dealing with people Opposites	Past forms and infinitives	Linkers Editing	Groups of consonants **Connected speech:** Linking sounds **Stress and intonation:** Questions	Management issues Listening practice
Unit 8 **Markets** page 32 / page 68	Words for talking about marketing	Adjectives: comparatives	E-mails	**Individual sounds:** The *schwa* sound **Connected speech:** Comparative forms **Stress and intonation:** Word stress	Meetings Listening practice
Unit 9 **Companies** page 36 / page 70	Words for talking about companies	Present continuous	Editing Company literature	Silent letters **Connected speech:** Pronouncing *are, aren't, isn't*	Talks and presentations Listening practice
Unit 10 **The Web** page 40 / page 72	Words for talking about the Internet Time expressions Prepositions	Future forms	Word order E-mails	**Individual sounds:** Pronouncing *v* and *w* **Connected speech:** Contracted forms **Stress and intonation:** Using stress to correct information	Making arrangements Listening practice
Unit 11 **Cultures** page 44 / page 74	Words for talking about cultures in countries and in companies	*should / shouldn't, could / would*	Linkers Topic sentences	Groups of consonants **Connected speech:** *Should* and *shouldn't* **Stress and intonation:** The *schwa* sound (unstressed syllables) Using stress to sound polite	Dialogues Listening practice
Unit 12 **Jobs** page 48 / page 76	Words for talking about jobs	Present perfect	Word order Job applications	**Individual sounds:** /ɒ/ and /ɔː/ **Connected speech:** Contractions	A job interview Listening practice

Answer key: page 78   **Audio scripts**: page 89

Introductions

Vocabulary

A **Reorder the letters to make names of countries.**

1 Cainh = ...China....
2 Risasu = ...
3 Sendew = ...
4 Planod = ...
5 Gyranem = ...
6 Aganirten = ...

B **Put in the missing letters to find the nationalities.**

1 Fadilah is Omani.
2 Mr Nakamura is J _ p _ n _ _ _ .
3 Christophe Boulan is F _ _ n _ h.
4 Ms Isabel Caceres is S _ _ ni _ h.
5 Andrew Harrison is E _ _ l _ _ h.
6 Vassiliki is G _ _ e _ .

C **Complete the crossword puzzle with names of countries or nationalities.**

Across

1 Sir Terry Leahy is the CEO of Tesco, the largest ..... supermarket chain. (7)
6 Ingvar Kamprad, founder of Ikea, is from ..... . (6)
8 ..... companies like Microsoft and GE are among the world's most respected companies. (2)
9 Toyota and Nissan are two carmakers from ..... . (5)
11 Lee Kun-hee is chairman of Samsung, the famous ..... technology company. (6)

Down

1 Natura, Petrobras and Weg are three companies from ..... . (6)
2 Lakshmi Mittal is from ..... . He is chief executive of Arcelor Mittal, the world's biggest steelmaker. (5)
3 Nestlé is one of the most famous ..... companies. (5)
4 Nokia, a ..... company, makes high-quality mobile phones. (7)
5 BMW, Porsche and Volkswagen are three carmakers from ..... . (7)
7 Jean-Paul Agon, L'Oréal's chief executive, is from ..... . (6)
10 British Airways, Virgin Atlantic and easyJet are airlines from the ..... . (2)

Vocabulary +

D Here are six adjectives. Write the names of the corresponding countries.

1 Danish   *Denmark*   4 Czech   ....
2 Dutch   ....   5 Turkish   ....
3 Pakistani ....   6 Senegalese ....

E Here are six countries. Write the corresponding adjectives.

1 Norway   *Norwegian*   4 Taiwan   ....
2 Portugal   ....   5 Slovakia   ....
3 Switzerland   ....   6 Thailand   ....

F Complete the groups below with the names of countries from the box and their corresponding nationality adjectives.

| ~~Bahrain~~ Chile Scotland Vietnam Iran Sudan Iraq Finland |

Group 1	
Adjectives ending in -an	
Country	**Nationality**
Brazil	Brazil**ian**
Germany	Germ**an**
....	....
....	....

Group 2	
Adjectives ending in -ish	
Country	**Nationality**
Poland	Pol**ish**
Spain	Span**ish**
....	....
....	....

Group 3	
Adjectives ending in -ese	
Country	**Nationality**
Japan	Japan**ese**
China	Chin**ese**
....	....
....	....

Group 4	
Adjectives ending in -i	
Country	**Nationality**
Kuwait	Kuwait**i**
Oman	Oman**i**
Bahrain	*Bahraini*
....	....

Language review

The verb *to be*

A Choose correct forms from the box to complete the sentences.

| am   'm   are   're   is   's |

1 Lucien and Marie-Claire ...*are*... our agents in Bordeaux.
2 Mrs Turner .... a programmer in Leeds.
3 My boss and I .... from Frankfurt.
4 Where .... your new assistant from?
5 Excuse me. .... you the new technician?
6 I .... Swiss, but my company .... Italian.
7 Dorota and Cezariusz .... Polish. Their office .... in Poznan.

B Put the appropriate form of the verb *to be* at the correct place(s) in each sentence.

1 His English very good.   *His English is very good.* .
2 Where they from?   ....
3 What her name?   ....
4 My office in Paris, but I not French.   ....
5 Mrs Lopez a lawyer.   ....
6 Alex and Rob from Italy.   ....

C Put the words in the correct order to make questions. You need one form from the box for each question.

am   are   is

1 your / Ingrid / name   *Is your name Ingrid?* .... ?
2 Spain / Isabel and Luis / from   .... ?
3 a / you / programmer   .... ?
4 Marketing / in / you and Tom   .... ?
5 I / tomorrow / in / Room 16   .... ?

D Match these sentence halves.

1 I'm in Sales,   **a)** but she isn't an accountant.
2 She's in Accounts,   **b)** so we aren't free.
3 My assistant and I are in a meeting all day,   **c)** so you aren't late.
    d) but you are very near the conference hall.
4 You aren't in the city centre,   **e)** but I'm not a salesman.
5 It's only 9:50,

E Write short answers to the questions.

1 Is Ákos from Turkey?
 No, he isn't. ... He's from Hungary.
2 Are you in Production too, Maria?
 .... I'm the assistant production manager.
3 Am I in room 243 tomorrow?
 .... You're in 112.
4 Am I late for the meeting?
 .... But just by five minutes, so don't worry.
5 Is Linda English too?
 .... She's from Australia.
6 Is the new sales assistant French?
 .... He's from Lyons.
7 Are you from Switzerland, Brigitte?
 .... I'm from Belgium.
8 Are you and Lucille in Marketing?
 .... We're both in Finance.

Language work

Writing
Editing

Ⓐ Beat the spellchecker! Use the correct word from the box to complete each of the sentences below.

| Is   is (x2)   from   football   are   ~~a~~ |

1 Is your wife _∧ *a* manager?

2 She married with two children.

3 Tom and Ana interested in travel.

4 Olympic Airways Greek?

5 My boss's favourite sport is.

6 The sales manager very busy today.

7 My best friend is Brazilian. He is Porto Seguro.

Ⓑ Put an apostrophe (') where necessary.

1 Her names Paola. *name's*

2 Akemis from Japan.

3 Her companys in Osaka.

4 Whats your job?

5 Its very modern, but it isnt very large.

6 'Are you and your colleague from Poland?'
 – 'No, we arent. Were from Ukraine.'

Ⓒ Rewrite the sentences, adding capital letters where necessary.

1 nikola is from croatia.   *Nikola is from Croatia*......

2 mrs kimura is japanese.   ....

3 is nokia danish?   ....

4 paul is married with two children.   ....

5 this is george ellis, from marketing. ....

6 mr brown's new boss is from london, ontario. ....

An e-mail

Ⓓ You are at an international trade fair in another country. You write an e-mail about the fair to a colleague in your office. Complete the e-mail with items from the box.

| a sales manager   business is   company sells   do business |
| ~~is a great city~~   is from Altheim |

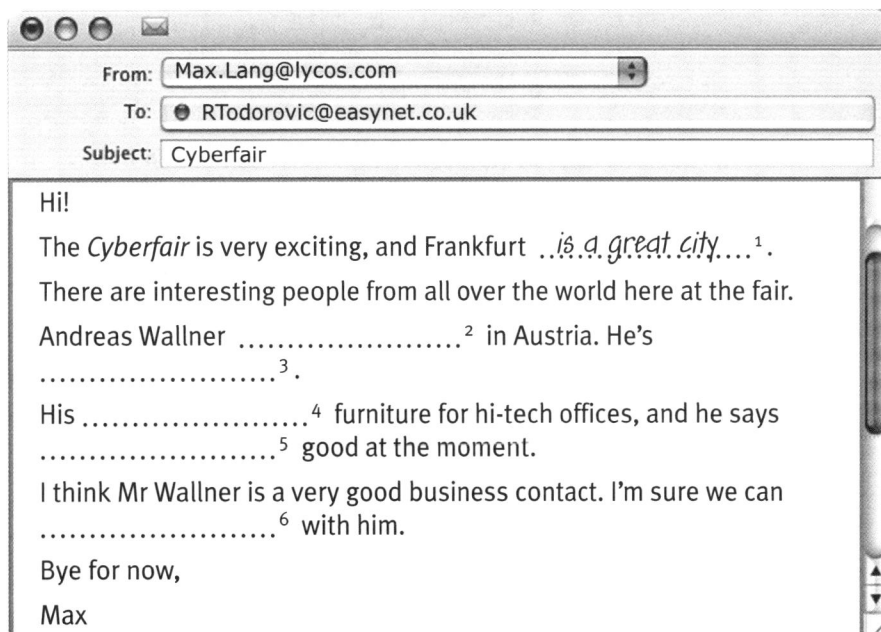

● ○ ○ ✉

From: Max.Lang@lycos.com

To: ● RTodorovic@easynet.co.uk

Subject: Cyberfair

Hi!

The *Cyberfair* is very exciting, and Frankfurt ..*is a great city*....[1].

There are interesting people from all over the world here at the fair.

Andreas Wallner ....[2] in Austria. He's

........................[3].

His ....[4] furniture for hi-tech offices, and he says

........................[5] good at the moment.

I think Mr Wallner is a very good business contact. I'm sure we can

........................[6] with him.

Bye for now,

Max

Work and leisure

Language work

Vocabulary

A Complete the sentences.

1 Tom says friendly colleagues are more important than a *high salary*.

2 I can start work at 7:30, 8:30 or 9:30. I'm really glad I can work
   f _ _ _ _ _ _ _ h _ _ _ _ .

3 Her job has a lot of t _ _ _ _ _ o _ _ _ _ _ _ _ _ _ _ _ _ . She goes to a
   different country every month!

4 When I travel on business, the company pays for my meals and my hotels.
   It's so easy when you have an e_ _ _ _ _ _ a _ _ _ _ _ _ .

5 My company has a gym, a swimming pool and many other s _ _ _ _ _
   f _ _ _ _ _ _ _ _ _ .

6 All our sales representatives use c _ _ _ _ _ _ c _ _ _ to visit customers in
   other cities.

7 I drive to work, so I'm glad my company has free p _ _ _ _ _ _ f _ _ _ _ _ _ _ _ _ _ .

8 For me, j _ _ s _ _ _ _ _ _ _ is what I need most. I have three children, so I
   don't want to be out of work.

B Write one letter in each empty box to make names of days, months or seasons.

1 | T | h | u | r | s | d | a | y |

2 | | | | | h | | | |

3 | | i | | | | |

4 | | | b | | | | | |

5 | | | | | d | | |

6 | | | t | | | |

C Complete the sentences with *at*, *in* or *on*.

1 Our departmental meeting is .. *on* ... Friday afternoon.

2 I don't like meetings .... the morning.

3 The first interview is .... 17 December.

4 The second interview is .... January.

5 When he travels all day, he can't sleep .... night.

6 She usually visits our head office .... the autumn.

7 They never work .... the weekend.

8 Are you free .... Wednesday?

9 Susan sometimes works .... Saturdays.

10 Do you often go out .... the evening?

11 He starts his first meeting .... 8:30.

D Write ⋀ to show the place of the missing word in each sentence. Write the word on the line.

1 Some of my colleagues love listening ⋀ hard rock.   ...*to*........

2 My boss and I don't like watching football TV.   ....

3 My colleagues and I often go to cinema on Saturdays.   ....

4 I quite like reading, but I hate to the radio.   ....

5 Our new secretary sometimes tennis at the weekend.   ....

6 How often do you go abroad holiday?   ....

Vocabulary +

E Complete the time phrases in the sentences with *at* or *in*. Write Ø if no word is missing.

1 Can I see you ...*Ø*.... next Tuesday?

2 They'll deliver the goods .... the end of the month.

3 We need to have a meeting .... this afternoon.

4 The office closes .... 6:00 p.m.

5 There's a staff party .... every December.

6 Our visitors arrive .... three hours' time.

7 She worked very hard .... last winter.

8 Hurry up! The bank closes .... ten minutes.

9 He travelled to China .... 1999.

10 I'm sorry. Mrs Moor's in a meeting .... the moment.

Discover the rule
Study the 10 sentences above and complete the rule.

We do **not** use *at* /*in* /*on* before *next*, ... , ... or .... in a time phrase.

F In each box, match the words that go together to find more things to do in your free time. Use a good dictionary to help you.

1 stay in	a) to an exhibition
2 play	b) a novel
3 read	c) a party
4 go	d) with your family
5 have	e) chess

6 listen	a) jogging
7 go for	b) a video
8 go	c) a walk
9 work in	d) to the radio
10 watch	e) the garden

Language review
Verb forms

A Complete the information about Kati Varga. Use the correct form of a verb from the box.

get	arrive	check	enjoy	go
have	have	spend	like	work

Kati Varga's working day

Kati Varga is the director of Commerzbank, a large bank in Budapest. She ...*gets*.¹ up at about 5:30 and usually goes jogging in the park. Then she ....² a shower and prepares breakfast for herself and her family. 'We all ....³ to have breakfast together,' she says, 'and that's great.'

She ....⁴ to work by metro. She ....⁵ at her office between 7:45 and 8 o'clock. Then she works at her desk for half an hour. 'I always ....⁶ my e-mail first thing every morning,' she says.

At 8:30 she starts her first meeting. She ....⁷ a lot of meetings in the morning with customers and also with other important bankers. 'I keep the afternoons free for staff meetings,' she says.

Two or three nights a week Ms Varga ....⁸ late at the office. She gets home late and often goes to bed after midnight.

She travels a lot and ....⁹ about 50 days abroad every year. In her free time, she likes hiking and playing tennis. 'And when the weather is nice, my family and I really ....¹⁰ sailing,' she says.

Word order

B Put the words in the correct order to make sentences.

1 She / a lot of / calls / every / makes / telephone / day.
She makes a lot of telephone calls every day.
2 In / evening, / watch / the / we / usually/ TV.
3 Tony /a / days / late / two / works / week.
4 How / you / often / do / visit / clients?
5 I / have / with / lunch / often / colleagues.
6 They / at / are / home / on / rarely / Saturdays.

C Match the words on the left with the words on the right to make expressions of time and frequency.

1 two	a) weekend
2 at the	b) to time
3 five	c) a week
4 from time	d) times a year
5 in the	e) then
6 now and	f) nights a week
7 once a	g) evening
8 twice	h) month

Writing
Spelling

A Complete the verbs in the following sentences.

1 Lucy go.*es*... to work by bus.
2 She arri......... at work at 8:45 a.m.
3 She star......... work at 9:00.
4 In the morning, she discu......... new plans with her colleagues.
5 She often h......... lunch in the staff cafeteria.
6 She enj......... her job a lot.
7 In the evening, she stu......... for her MBA.

Focus on capital letters

B **Rewrite the sentences, using capital letters where necessary.**

1 vera works till 5:30 on thursdays.
   Vera works till 5:30 on Thursdays.

2 she goes to the uk every year in march.

3 paul sometimes reads the *financial times*.

4 they live in amsterdam, but they aren't dutch.

5 their office is in oxford street.

6 as you know, i work for the european commission.

7 the polish representatives arrive at heathrow at 7:30 a.m.

8 louise and bill are from the united states.

9 how often do you watch the bbc?

Filling in a form

C **Read the text and complete the form below.**

Hello! My name's Raoul Gautier and I'm the PR[1] Manager with the Banque de l'Ouest.

It's a new job for me, and I like it very much.

My address is 47, Avenue Aristide Briand, Toulouse, and my phone number is 55 78 43 00.

I'm twenty-four years old – the same age as my partner Sarah. We're getting married next year!

[1] PR is short for Public Relations

First name: ....*Raoul*..............

Surname: ....

Age: ....

Marital status: Single/Married

Occupation: ....

Address: ....

....

Telephone number: ....

An e-mail

D **Raoul Gautier is the new PR Manager with the Banque de l'Ouest in Toulouse. Put the sentences in the best order to write his e-mail to the staff.**

From: RGautier@banqueouest.fr
To: staff@banqueouest.fr
Subject:

Dear All,

a) I also have to give them information about our work.   1 | b |

b) This is just to introduce myself.   2 | |

c) I look forward to meeting you all at our staff meeting on Friday.   3 | |

d) My main responsibility is to communicate with the public and the media.   4 | |

e) My name is Raoul Gautier and I am the new PR Manager.   5 | |

With best wishes,

Raoul Gautier

3 Problems

Vocabulary **A** **Complete the sentences.**

1 Flight FR42 is d _e l a y e d_ by half an hour because of bad weather. We apologise for the inconvenience.

2 The photos aren't in the envelope. They're m _ _ _ _ _ _ .

3 Nobody knows where the report is. It's l _ _ _ .

4 Don't sit on that chair! It's b _ _ _ _ _ .

5 Let's take a taxi. We don't want to be l _ _ _ for the meeting.

too / enough **B** **Match each sentence on the left with a sentence on the right.**

1 I think Alpha Tours is too expensive.

2 It's too far to walk.

3 The office is really too small.

4 The interviewer talks too fast.

5 There isn't enough information in this report.

6 They say the Royal Hotel isn't good enough.

7 This machine's too slow.

a) We need more detail.

b) Please book my flight with a different company.

c) It takes three minutes to make 10 copies.

d) Let's take a taxi.

e) It's difficult to understand her.

f) There isn't enough space for all the staff.

g) They want to stay at the Astoria.

too / enough / *very* **C** **Correct the sentences that are wrong.**

1 I can afford to buy the LJ200 printer, but it's ~~too~~ expensive. *very*

2 This mobile phone is too big to fit in my pocket.

3 It's too late to telephone. They close at 5:30.

4 Come to our country! The food is delicious and the people are too friendly.

5 My boss is great, and my colleagues are too nice.

6 I can't do it enough fast. I need some help.

Vocabulary + **D** **Match these adjectives with their opposites. Use a good dictionary to help you.**

1 boring

2 difficult

3 dirty

4 dishonest

5 expensive

6 inefficient

7 negative

8 old-fashioned

9 unpleasant

10 weak

a) cheap

b) clean

c) strong

d) efficient

e) honest

f) interesting

g) modern

h) pleasant

i) positive

j) easy

E **Complete each sentence with the best word.**

1 Can you help, please? These instructions are too ...*b*... for me to understand.

   a) unpleasant **b)** difficult **c)** dirty

2 It's very .... of them to say they've made a big mistake.

   a) easy **b)** inefficient **c)** honest

3 Renata always does a lot of work, and she works so fast! She's very ...., isn't she?

   a) modern **b)** positive **c)** efficient

4 The trade show was really exciting, but the speech at the beginning was quite ....

   a) boring **b)** cheap **c)** interesting

5 The .... dollar made many US products cheaper than those from Japan.

   a) dishonest **b)** weak **c)** dirty

6 Tickets for the concert are too .... Let's take our visitors to a restaurant instead.

   a) easy **b)** expensive **c)** difficult

7 You always say business is not very good. Come on, try to be a bit more ....

   a) positive **b)** negative **c)** old-fashioned

Language review

Negatives and questions

A **Write the opposite of these sentences.**

1 They report to the director. *They don't report to the director.*

2 She doesn't start very early. *She starts very early.*

3 She finishes work late.

4 We don't often work at the weekend.

5 They sell office equipment.

6 I make a lot of phone calls.

7 He doesn't write reports.

B **Study the information in the table. Then complete the sentences.**

	Kate and Ross	Jim
1 Do you often travel abroad?	✘	✔
2 Do you get lots of e-mails?	✔	✘
3 Do you have regular breaks?	✘	✔
4 Do you attend a lot of meetings?	✔	✘
5 Do you often entertain foreign visitors?	✘	✔
6 Do you read the *Financial Times*?	✔	✘

1 Kate and Ross ...*don't often travel abroad*... .

2 Jim .... e-mails.

3 Jim .... breaks.

4 Kate and Ross .... meetings.

5 Kate and Ross .... visitors.

6 Jim .... the *Financial Times*.

Language work

C Study the information in exercise B again. Then complete the sentences, as in the example.

1 Kate and Ross don't often travel abroad, *but Jim does* .

   NOT ~~Kate and Ross don't often travel abroad but Jim often travels abroad.~~

2 Kate and Ross .... lots of e-mails, but ....

3 Kate and Ross .... regular breaks, but ....

4 Jim .... a lot of meetings, but ....

5 Jim often .... visitors, but ....

6 .... the *Financial Times*, but .... doesn't.

D Complete the sentences with *a*, *some* or *any*.

1 We've got *some* problems with cash flow this month.

2 Joe's office has got air conditioning, but it hasn't got .... windows.

3 The invoice is incorrect. Please send us .... new one.

4 My new office hasn't got .... very nice view.

5 Have you got .... meetings on Tuesday?

6 We haven't got .... information about the missing documents.

7 Has he got .... problems with the new boss?

8 Please give us .... details.

9 They haven't got .... Korean customers.

10 Ms Torres has got .... meetings on Friday, but she's free on Monday.

Writing

Spelling

Tip

When you write a business letter or a report, always use the full forms.

A Write out the full forms.

1 We'd like to inform you that there's a problem with the printer.
   We would like to inform you that there is a problem with the printer.

2 Their company's got a cash flow problem.

3 Our order's delayed.

4 It doesn't work properly.

5 It's very efficient.

6 She hasn't got an assistant.

Focus on punctuation

B Separate the words and punctuate the sentences. Use capital letters where necessary.

1 healwayssendshisreportsontime
   He always sends his reports on time.

2 theypayalotofrentforasmallofficeinthecitycentre

3 whendoesthemeetingfinish

4 billhasgotalargeoffice,buthehasnotgotacompanycar

5 howmanypeopledotheyemploy

Linking information: *and* or *but*?

C Match these sentence halves. Then link them with *and* or *but*.

1 He is a good team player,
2 She is always on time,
3 The new machine is small,
4 The report is very long,
5 There are a lot of changes,
6 Our office is small,

a) it is very heavy.
b) it is very easy to understand.
c) she is very efficient.
d) it is in the city centre.
e) he does not go to meetings.
f) staff are worried about their jobs.

1 *He is a good team player, but he does not go to meetings.*

A letter **D** **Complete the letter with the words from the box.**

damaged	inform	missing	~~October~~	problem	send

Language work

SIMONS SECURITY SERVICES

Manor Road, Holdenby, Northampton NN8 9TJ

David Ashby
Crawley Electronics
27 Old London Road
Benson
Oxon OX10 3RL

15 _October_ ¹

Dear Mr Ashby

Subject: our order Ref. PJ/66

We would like to ....² you that we have a ....³ with the printer you delivered this morning.

The box is ....⁴ and there is a piece ....⁵ (Ref. No. ASD32/S).

In addition, there is no instruction manual.

Could you please ....⁶ us the missing part and the manual as soon as possible.

We look forward to hearing from you.

Yours sincerely

Jane Warren

Product Manager

Have you noticed?

The box is damaged. There is a piece missing. There is no instruction manual.

Notice how you can **link** this information:

The box is damaged **and** there is a piece missing. **In addition,** there is no instruction manual.

E **Make sentences using the linkers in the same way.**

1 The office is small. The office is crowded. The air conditioning does not work.

2 The screen is small. The picture is not very good. There is no remote control.

3 The photocopier does not work. There is only one phone line. The receptionist is never on time.

Travel

Vocabulary

A Use the clues to complete the crossword puzzle.

Across

1 Can I take this as hand ....? (7)

5 Going through .... checks sometimes takes a long time. (8)

6 Travelling is OK, but I hate .... all those suitcases before the trip! (7)

9 Mr Komano .... at 16:45. I'll go and pick him up at the airport. (7)

12 All Paris trains .... from platform 8. (5)

Down

2 Passengers for flight BA247 to São Paulo, please go to 71. (4)

3 Have you got any ....-free goods? (4)

4 A .... ticket to the city centre, please. (6)

7 Could I have an .... call at 5:30 a.m. tomorrow, please? (5)

8 Please .... your seatbelts and switch off any electronic devices. (6)

10 You are in .... 12, seat B. (3)

11 Would you like an aisle or a window ....? (4)

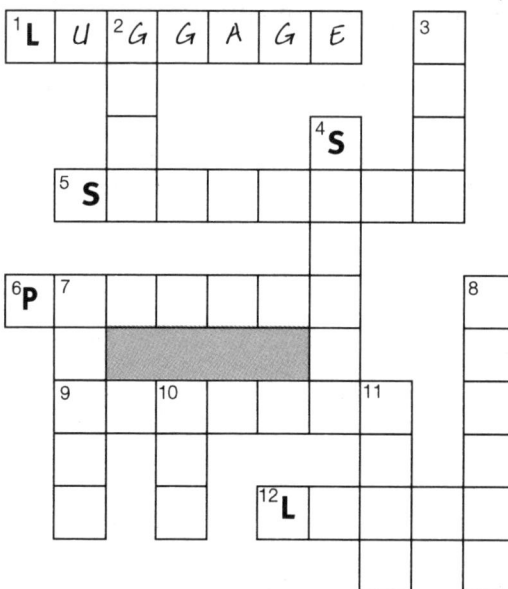

Collocations

B Cross out the word that has no partner.

1

to make
to change
to do
to confirm

a reservation

2

a room
your ticket
a flight
your luggage

to book

3

to queue
to reserve
to buy
to change

a ticket

4

at an airport
at a hotel
at reception
a platform

to check in

Vocabulary +

C **Complete the sentences with words from the box.**

at (x3) by (x2) for from (x2) off on to (x5)

1 A lot of my colleagues go to work ...by... car.
2 I go to the office .... foot. It takes me 35 minutes.
3 Sometimes, I go .... bus. That takes me about 20 minutes.
4 I get .... the bus at the City Park, then I walk .... the office.
5 I start work .... 9:00, but I like to arrive .... the office early.
6 How long does it take to get .... here .... your office?
7 The plane arrives .... 2:20.
8 It's a great airport. You never wait very long .... your luggage.
9 Passengers for flight BA784 .... Rome, please go .... Gate 36.
10 Could you book me a room .... 30 August .... 3 September, please?

D **Make pairs of opposites. Use a good dictionary to help you.**

1 to land   **a)** to arrive
2 to leave   **b)** to be on time
3 to get off   **c)** to take off
4 to be delayed   **d)** to miss
5 to catch   **e)** to get on

E **Complete the sentences with the correct form of an item from exercise D.**

1 There is sometimes a last security check just before the plane .takes off... .
2 Be polite, and wait for people to .... the train before you ....
3 Don't .... the 8:30 Intercity! The next one isn't until 11:00.
4 Right. So departure time is 4:25. And what time does it .... ?
5 We regret to announce that all trains .... because of the snow.

Language review

can

A **Put the questions in the right column according to the meaning of *can*.**

can (ability)	*can* (permission)	*can* (what is possible)
2		1

1 Can we fly direct from Rome to Tashkent?
2 Can you use the new photocopier?
3 Can she speak Russian?
4 Can I use your computer for half an hour or so, please?
5 Where can I buy phone cards?
6 Excuse me. Can I open the window?
7 Can you hear me now?
8 Can I just make a phone call, please?
9 Can we go to the airport by underground?

B **Match the answers to the questions in exercise A.**

a) Yes. You don't need to change. `1`

b) Yes, you can. But you need to change twice from here. `9`

c) At the post office. A lot of kiosks sell them, too. ☐

d) Sure! It's really hot in here. ☐

e) Yes, go ahead. Just dial 9 to get an outside line. ☐

f) Yes, of course. You can use it all morning if you like. I'll be in a meeting. ☐

g) Yes, that's better. It's not a very good line, is it? ☐

h) No, I can't. But I want to learn. ☐

i) Yes. And her Chinese is quite good, too. ☐

there is, there are

C **Complete the sentences with the correct form (+, –, ?) of *there is* or *there are*.**

1 The area is a bit boring. *There isn't* anywhere to go after 7:00 in the evening.

2 What can we do? .... a very long queue at the ticket office.

3 .... any direct flights to Brussels on Tuesdays or Thursdays, I'm afraid.

4 I'm afraid .... a small problem with your reservation, sir.

5 It's great! .... lots of shops near our hotel.

6 .... a fitness centre at the Victoria Hotel?

7 Oh dear! .... any meeting rooms available next week.

8 .... Internet access in each room?

9 I think .... two direct flights a day.

10 It's an excellent hotel, but .... a swimming pool.

Language +

there and *it*

D **Complete the sentences with *there* or *it*.**

1 *There* 's another flight at 10:15. *It* 's a Lufthansa flight.

2 'Is .... a gift shop?' 'Yes, madam. .... 's on the first floor.'

3 .... 's too late. .... 's nobody at the office.

4 I know the Astoria. .... 's an excellent hotel. And .... 's very near the airport.

5 .... 's Internet access in each room, and .... 's free.

6 Szeged? I just know .... 's a city in Hungary. But what kind of place is .... ? Is .... anywhere to go in the evening?

Writing

Editing

A **Beat the spellchecker! Use the correct word from the box to complete each of the sentences below.**

confirm ~~double~~ from like are station

        double
1 Do you want a single or a ∧ room?

2 I'd like to book a room Sunday 5th to Thursday 9th of this month.

3 I'm ringing to my flight details.

4 Would you an aisle or a window seat?

5 Can we meet at the railway at 8:30?

6 There two restaurants where you can entertain business guests.

A hotel reservation

B **Complete the two faxes with words from the box.**

available	bath	~~book~~	confirm	cost	inform	look
	Please	sincerely	Thank			

C r a w l e y E l e c t r o n i c s

F A X

From: Crawley Electronics   +44 1865 896442
To: Hotel Belfort, Crolles (France)   +33 4 76 05 06 77

I would like to ...._book_...¹ one single room with ....² for Mr Paul Wilberg, our General Manager, for two nights from Wednesday 2 September.

..............³ let us know how much the room costs per night, including full breakfast.

..............⁴ you for confirming this by fax.

Liz Stamford

Hotel Belfort
Crolles, (France)

FAX
From: Hotel Belfort, Crolles (France)   +33 4 76 05 06 77
To: Crawley Electronics   +44 1865 896442

Dear Ms Stamford

Thank you for your fax.

We are pleased to ....⁵ you that we have a single room with bath ....⁶ for two nights from 2 September. The ....⁷ is 85 euros, inclusive of breakfast.

We can ....⁸ that the room is reserved for Mr Paul Wilberg.

We ....⁹ forward to seeing Mr Wilberg in September.

Yours ....¹⁰

Guy Lefranc

Hotel Belfort

Language work

Food and entertaining

Vocabulary **A** Complete the text with the best words.

How to make your business guests happy

Today, you don't ..b....[1] business only in your office. All over the world, people understand that it is important to ....[2] business partners, customers and suppliers. When you plan to eat ....[3] with your visitors, there are a few rules to remember.

First, don't take them to a restaurant that nobody knows! You want a place with a pleasant atmosphere, ...[4] food and efficient ....[5]. So if you do not know where to go, ask your friends and colleagues to ....[6] a restaurant.

Secondly, choose a restaurant with a varied ....[7] so everybody can find a ....[8] they like or want to try. Remember too that some of your guests may be ....[9].

Finally, relax and be open to cultural differences. Some people are very happy with just a main ....[10] and do not want to spend a lot of time over lunch or dinner. Others like big ....[11] and expect aperitif, starter, main course, dessert and coffee!

1 **a)** work   **b)** do   **c)** make
2 **a)** entertain   **b)** party   **c)** have fun
3 **a)** in   **b)** up   **c)** out
4 **a)** taste   **b)** delicious **c)** right
5 **a)** chef   **b)** waiter   **c)** service
6 **a)** recommend   **b)** inform   **c)** advise
7 **a)** menu   **b)** card   **c)** bill
8 **a)** food   **b)** dish   **c)** cook
9 **a)** diet   **b)** receipts **c)** vegetarians
10 **a)** course   **b)** food   **c)** pie
11 **a)** eats   **b)** meals   **c)** breakfasts

B Use the clues to complete the crossword puzzle.

Across

2 A river and sea fish. (6)
4 A sea fish. (3)
6 It's Italian. It's a pasta dish. (9)
7 Meat from a young sheep. (4)
9 Things like apples and bananas. (5)

Down

1 It's very popular as a starter. (4)
3 Vegetarians do not eat it. (4)
5 It's Italian. It's popular as a type of fast food all over the world. (5)
6 A mixture of vegetables, eaten cold. (5)
8 Meat from a cow. (4)

Crossword: 2 across SALMON; 4 D; 6 P; Z; D; 9 F

Vocabulary +

C Match the following 'food words' to their definitions. Use a good dictionary to help you.

1 barbecue
2 buffet
3 couscous
4 kebab
5 mousse
6 risotto

a) a dessert made from cream and eggs and often flavoured with chocolate

b) a dish of small pieces of meat and vegetables cooked on a metal stick

c) a meal in which people serve themselves from a table and often eat standing up

d) a typical dish from North Africa made from semolina and often served with meat and a lot of vegetables

e) an Italian dish of rice cooked with vegetables, meat or fish

f) an outdoor meal when food is cooked over an open fire

Collocations

D Cross out the word that has no partner.

1
to have
to order
to call
to buy

some food

2
to bake

bread
soup
potatoes
cakes

3
grilled

salad
fish
meat
chicken

4
to taste

food
a dish
a receipt
a drink

5
to recommend

a restaurant
a dish
a bill
a book

Language review

Countable and uncountable nouns

A Put the words in the correct column.

restaurant	beef	credit card	fish	hamburger
	money	soup	waiter	

Countable	Uncountable
1 restaurant	5
2	6
3	7
4	8

B Copy each sentence into the correct box.

singular countable noun	plural countable noun	uncountable noun
+ I'd like a dessert.	+	+
–	–	–
?	?	?

I'd like **a** dessert.
Are there **any** green apples?
I don't want **a** large glass.
I'd like **some** chips.
I'd like **some** soup.

Is there **a** Chinese restaurant in town?
Is there **any** meat in it?
There aren't **any** tables free.
We haven't got **any** milk.

much, many **C** Complete the sentences with *much* or *many*.

1 There aren't ..*many*.. rice dishes on the menu.

2 How .... tables do we need to reserve for the staff party?

3 That's not a very exciting menu. There isn't .... choice, is there?

4 Let's go to another restaurant. There are too .... people here.

5 How .... food do we need for the buffet lunch?

6 There isn't .... to do for the reception[1]. Philip organises everything.

7 There's too .... salt in this soup. I can't eat it.

8 Their food is always excellent, but they don't have .... desserts.

> [1] *reception:* a big formal party to celebrate a special event or to welcome an important visitor.

D Study these sentences.

I drink **a lot of** milk.

We need **a lot of** vegetables.

What's the rule?

- In positive sentences, *a lot of* is more usual than *much /many*, especially in spoken English.
- *Much /many* are more usual in negative sentences and in questions.

Match the first and second parts of the sentences.

1 They don't eat much meat,

2 They have a lot of fish dishes,

3 We make a lot of fresh fruit juice,

4 I don't go to Indian restaurants much,

5 He has a lot of money,

6 I need a lot of eggs,

7 We don't buy many sweet things,

a) but I go to pizzerias a lot.

b) but we don't buy many soft drinks.

c) but he never invites many people to his parties.

d) but they haven't got many starters.

e) but sometimes we eat a lot of chocolate.

f) but I don't need much milk.

g) but they eat a lot of vegetables.

Writing

Editing

A Read this review of the White Lake Restaurant.

In each line **1–7** there is **one wrong word**.

For each line, **underline the wrong word** in the text and **write the correct word** in the space provided.

You can entertain <u>you</u> guests in a beautiful setting at the White
Lake Restaurant. In the heart of Belleville Forest, just ten minute
away from the city centre by public transport or by car, he has
excellent parking facilities. At a White Lake Restaurant, you can enjoy
delicious fish dish from our region, as well as a wide range of
vegetarian and meet dishes. It is a popular place, so you need to
booking a table in advance. It is quite expensive, but it is worth a visit.

1 ...*your*........

2 ....

3 ....

4 ....

5 ....

6 ....

7 ....

A message **B** Put the sentences in this telephone message in the right order.

TELEPHONE MESSAGE

For: *the Restaurant Manager*
From: *Liz Stamford of Crawley Electronics 01865 896 442*
Date: *12 Nov.*

a) *It's for a group of 18, including 14 Chinese visitors.*
b) *Ms Stamford wants to book one of our dining rooms for Friday evening, 22 Nov.*
c) *So can we do a three-course meal with a lot of regional specialities?*
d) *We also need to quote her a price (drinks included) before 15 Nov.*
e) *The others want to try typical dishes from our region.*
f) *There are three vegetarians in the group.*

☐
1
☐
☐
☐
☐

C Complete the fax with words from the box.

vegetarian Yours confirm menu again ~~pleased~~ book

The White Lake Restaurant
FAX

From: J Richards, Restaurant Manager   +44 (0) 1279 677 899
To: Ms L Stamford, Crawley Electronics   +44 (0) 1865 896442

13 November
Dear Ms Stamford

Thank you for your enquiry of 12 November.

We are ...*pleased*...[1] to inform you that you can ....[2] our exclusive Viennese Dining Room for 22 November from 7 p.m. It can seat up to 25 people and has a beautiful view of the lake.

On the next page you can find a sample ....[3]. It has a lot of typical dishes, including some regional fish dishes and ....[4] specialities.

Please let us know what you think.

The price for a three-course meal (vegetarian or standard) would be £40 per person, including drinks and 10% service.

For first-time customers like you, there is a special offer: you can choose anything from our desserts menu completely free of charge, as well as tea or coffee.

Could you please ....[5] your booking by 17 November.

Thank you once ....[6] for your enquiry.

We look forward to seeing you and your guests on 22 November.

...............[7] sincerely

J Richards

Sales

Vocabulary

A **Complete the text with the best words.**

When buyers ...*C*..¹ an order with a seller for the first time, they usually have a lot of questions.

First, they want to ....² prices, of course, and they also want to know what kind of ....³ the seller can offer.

Very often, buyers also ask if the seller has the goods in ....⁴, and if he or she can deliver on ....⁵.

Sometimes, buyers will ask if it is possible to pay in ....⁶. If the seller agrees, he or she will often expect buyers to pay a ....⁷.

1 **a)** put	**b)** take	**c)** place
2 **a)** compare	**b)** offer	**c)** say
3 **a)** commission	**b)** discount	**c)** feature
4 **a)** shop	**b)** stock	**c)** delivery
5 **a)** delay	**b)** speed	**c)** time
6 **a)** instalments	**b)** parts	**c)** shares
7 **a)** deposit	**b)** cheque	**c)** guarantee

B **Use the clues to complete the crossword puzzle.**

Across

2 At *Dart Car Hire* the .... can get some deals for half price. (5)

4 When you bring the car back, we e-mail you a detailed .... (7)

7 It doesn't cost extra for insurance. It's .... (4)

9 As a *Dart Car Hire Gold Club* member, you get free hire days or airline miles as your .... (6)

10 Club members also enjoy many other exclusive .... (8)

Down

1 Be quick! Our offer is for a limited .... only. (6)

3 At *Dart Car Hire* you don't queue when you .... the car – we e-mail you all the information. (6)

5 As a *Dart Car Hire Gold Club* member, you can .... your own car. (6)

6 You can pay over a 12-month period. We offer interest-free .... (6)

8 If you hire a Mini or a Smart car, you can .... up to 50%. (4)

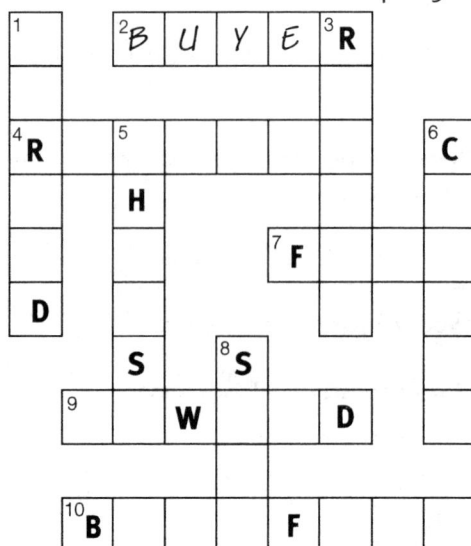

Vocabulary +

Collocations

C Cross out the word that has no partner.

1   to offer — to get — a discount — to give — ~~to place~~

2   to pay — to lose — a deposit — to fax — to ask for

3   to pay — to order — goods — to deliver — to return

4   to promote — to receive — an order — to place — to cancel

5   to ask for — to give — a guarantee — to say — to provide

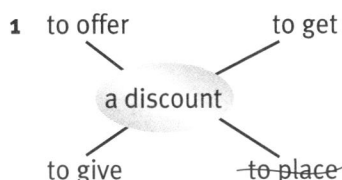

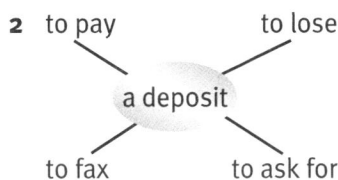

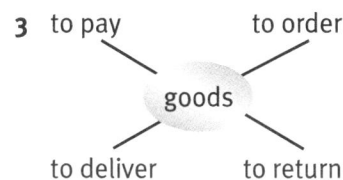

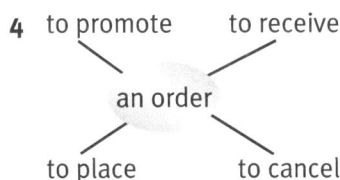

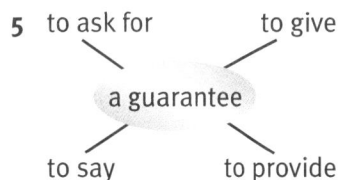

D Match each word or phrase to its definition.

1 after-sales service
2 guarantee period
3 retail
4 wholesale
5 supplier
6 competitor

a) a company or a person that provides a particular type of product
b) help, advice or free repairs that you get after you buy a product
c) a person who tries to be more successful than you
d) the selling of goods to businesses, usually in large quantities
e) time when the seller repairs or replaces a product free of charge
f) the selling of goods to the public, usually through shops

E Complete each sentence with a word or phrase from exercise D.

1 Lantex never delivers on time. We have to look for another .. *supplier* .... .

2 Our products are available in department stores and other .... outlets.

3 Sales are very good, but our main .... 's sales are also going up very quickly.

4 Ten percent discount and a two-year .... ! That's really a very good offer.

5 We are in the .... trade and sell our clothes to retailers and fashion houses.

6 If you have a problem with the machine, just contact our .... department.

Language review
Past forms

A Complete the sentences with *was* or *were*.

1 Sandra .. *was* .. at the meeting.
2 Jeff and Liz .... at Head Office yesterday.
3 There .... a lot of sales representatives at the meeting.
4 It .... difficult to get a discount.
5 The people .... nice, but their questions .... very difficult. Or maybe I .... just a bit tired.
6 The product presentation .... last Tuesday. My boss and I .... there to talk about our new brand of soft drinks.
7 Their products .... always the best on the market.
8 Two or three of our customers from Korea .... there.

Language work

B Complete the verb forms.

Infinitive	Past
1 buy	b _ough_ t
2 c _ _ _	cost
3 fly	fl _ _
4 get	g _ _
5 g _ _ _	gave

Infinitive	Past
6 pay	p _ _ _
7 s _ _ _	sold
8 spend	sp _ _ _
9 t _ _ _	took
10 write	wr _ _ _

C Complete the sentences with a past form. Use verbs from exercise B.

1 Last month, we ..*bought*.. ten new computers for our administrative staff.

2 I .... a memo to all reps yesterday.

3 He .... up at 9:00, so of course he was late for the meeting.

4 Our company .... a lot on promotion last year.

5 They .... for everything in cash.

6 We .... back to Zurich with Lufthansa.

D Complete the information about the sales figures with the past form of the verbs given.

Last year's overall sales figures ..*were*..[1] excellent for Nielsen Electronics. In January, they ....[2] the RU20 CD player, and sales ....[3] up from 2,000 to 2,500 the next month.	be introduce go
In March, sales ....[4] 3,500.	reach
Sales then ....[5] at the same level through the next quarter, but they ....[6] to go up in July and August, when they ....[7] to 4,000.	stay continue increase
Nielsen ....[8] to launch their digital camcorder, the DCC-N300, in September, but production problems ....[9] the introduction of this new model.	want delay
So Nielsen ....[10] it at the end of October. Overall sales ....[11] down after August, and at the end of October they were at 3,500.	launch go
However, the DCC-N300 ....[12] very popular, and the overall volume of sales ....[13] until the end of the year, when it ....[14] 4,500.	be grow reach

E Use the information in exercise D to draw the approximate pattern of overall sales.

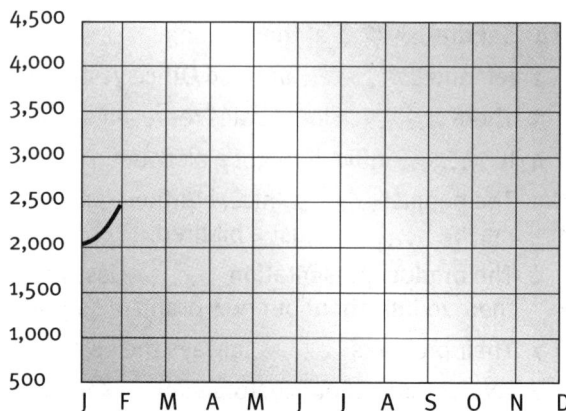

Writing
Editing

A Beat the spellchecker! Use the correct word from the box to complete each of the sentences below.

~~be~~	a	deposit	address	ask	for

1 Salespeople have to *be* clear what their objectives are.
2 Before they place an order, a lot of people like to questions.
3 Please quote us price for the goods listed below.
4 This special promotion is only a short time.
5 Unfortunately, we wrote the wrong delivery on the package.
6 We paid a €200 and the rest in 12 monthly instalments.

B Read this job advertisement.

In each line **1–6** there is **one wrong word**.
For each line, **underline the wrong word** in the text and **write the correct word** in the space provided.

We are a medium-sized cosmetics <u>an</u> toiletries company based in Victoria.

Last year we increased our sales by 20% and launch several new products.

At present we are expanding our sale force, creating opportunities throughout

the country for experience sales representatives. Our sales representatives

manage their own areas and help customers to promote our brands. They showing

customers how to increase sales. The advise customers on equipment,

advertising and special promotions.

1 ...*and*...
2 ....
3 ....
4 ....
5 ....
6 ....

A letter

C Put the sentences in this letter in the correct order, 1–8.

Medea Discos
Baixos 482
08030 Barcelona
SPAIN

25 February

1	Dear Mrs Gutierrez,
☐	Thank you once again for your order, and we hope we can be of service in the future.
☐	The CD and cassette shelving system you ordered is ready.
☐	Yours sincerely,
☐	We are now making arrangements for shipment to Barcelona.
☐	Thank you for your order No. 554S of 11th February.
☐	We look forward to further orders from you.
☐	You may therefore expect delivery by the end of the month.

L. Destrée

Univers Etagères

35, rue Planterose
33000 Bordeaux
FRANCE

People

Vocabulary

A **Complete the sentences with the correct adjectives about people.**

1 Tim is a very *qu* i *et* person. He never says anything in meetings.

2 Pierre likes going to parties and meeting new people. He's extremely _ _ _ ia _ _ _ .

3 Our new manager has lots of new ideas, and she always finds good solutions to problems. She's very _ _ _ at _ _ _ .

4 You're late again. Could you try to be a bit more _ _ _ ct _ _ _ ?

5 I am _ _ _ _ t _ _ _ _ and I would really like to become head of my department one day.

6 Lucy is very _ _ _ d-w _ _ _ _ _ _ . She works longer hours than everyone else.

B **Complete the sentences with words from the box. Write Ø if no word is missing.**

| with (x2)   on   for (x2)   to   at |

1 A motivating manager encourages ...*Ø*.... employees to work well.

2 A sales rep should never be rude .... customers.

3 Heinz is very helpful. He likes to do things .... other people.

4 Sandra always meets .... deadlines.

5 Claudia is very practical. She is really good .... making things work.

6 Sakiko is never late .... meetings.

7 I like working in a team and I get on well .... others.

8 A good employee always arrives .... time.

9 He was nice, but he was not very popular .... his colleagues.

10 Their new manager really knows how to motivate .... staff.

C **Match the sentence halves to make definitions for the new adjectives about people.**

1 A decisive person
2 A confident person
3 An efficient person
4 An energetic person
5 An enthusiastic person
6 A reliable person

a) is very active and does not feel tired quickly.

b) can make quick decisions in a difficult situation.

c) does not let you down.

d) believes that they can be successful.

e) can do tasks well without wasting time.

f) shows a lot of interest and excitement.

Opposites

D Write the opposite of the adjectives in the box in the correct column.

~~enthusiastic~~   ~~decisive~~   efficient   patient   polite   reliable   sociable

un-	in-	im-
unenthusiastic	*indecisive*	....
....	....	....
....		

Language review

Past forms and infinitives

A Complete the verb forms.

Infinitive	Past		Infinitive	Past
1 begin	b _ _ _ n		6 find	f _ _ _ _
2 br _ _ _	brought		7 go	_ _ _ _
3 catch	ca _ _ _ _		8 know	_ _ _ w
4 come	c _ _ _		9 l _ _ _ _	left
5 _ _ _ _ _	drove		10 send	s _ _ _

B Choose the correct verb form from exercise A to complete the sentences.

1 I didn't .*know*.. that you .*went*.. on a training course last month.

2 I didn't .... to work because of the snow. I .... a bus instead.

3 Why did Emma .... the company?

4 Did he .... the report by post, or did he .... it here himself?

5 When did the training course .... ?

6 Our first manager really .... how to motivate us, didn't he?

7 I didn't .... to the staff meeting. I was feeling very ill.

8 This is very useful information. Where did you .... it?

9 Did you .... the early morning train?

10 Why didn't Peter .... into partnership with Koreka Media?

C Now match these responses to the sentences in exercise B.

a) He certainly did. We all wanted to work hard for the company. [6]

b) He delivered it by hand yesterday afternoon. [ ]

c) Well, he heard that they were in financial difficulty. [ ]

d) It was all in last year's annual report. [ ]

e) No, I didn't. I came by car. [ ]

f) On 26 February. [ ]

g) Really? I thought everyone in the office knew! [ ]

h) Well, I think she didn't get on with the new manager. [ ]

i) Were you? Did you see a doctor? [ ]

j) Yeah. I left my car at home too. [ ]

D Put the words in the questions in the correct order.

1 they / punctual / Were / ?   *Were they punctual?*

2 a / Did / he / in / like / team / to / work / ?

3 they / Were / hard-working / ?

4 colleagues / her / popular / Mrs Whitehead / Was / with / ?

5 motivate / know / Did / how / people / she / to / ?

6 happy / Sandra / to / Were / with / work / you / ?

Language work

E Match these short answers to the questions in exercise D.

a) Yes, they were. ☐ *1*

b) No, she wasn't. ☐

c) Yes, she did. ☐

d) No, he didn't. ☐

e) Yes, I was. ☐

f) No, they weren't. ☐

F Complete the short answers to the questions.

1 Was Philip on time? No, ...*he wasn't*..... .

2 Did you and Barbara go to the staff party? No, ...

3 Did the sales reps get all the information
   they need? .... did.

4 Were Sue and Tom in the same team? .... weren't.

5 Does Sue work in the research team? No, ...

6 Was the training course useful? Yes, ...

7 Were the participants satisfied? Yes, ...

8 Can you meet this deadline? Yes, ...

G Read the text. Then make questions for the answers below.

Profile

Birgitte Nielsen was born in Aarhus, but her parents moved to Copenhagen when she was only three years old.

She was a very successful student. Her favourite subjects were Physics and Maths. In fact, she was always very good with numbers, maybe because her father worked in a bank and her mother was a computer programmer.

At the age of 18, Birgitte wrote a book called *FORTRAN for Beginners*.

The students liked it a lot and said it was better than the course book!

After secondary school, she went to Dublin for a few years, where she did an MBA. Her two passions, computer programming and business, led her to found her own company at the age of twenty-five. Today, Nielsen Electronics is a very successful business, with branches in five different European countries.

1 In Aarhus.

   Where was Birgitte born?

2 To Copenhagen.

3 Yes, she was.

4 Physics and Maths.

5 In a bank.

6 Yes, they liked it a lot.

7 In Dublin.

8 She founded Nielsen Electronics.

9 Yes, it is.

10 Five.

Writing

Linkers

A Complete the sentences with the correct linker from the box.

because (x4)　　but (x2)　　so (x2)

1 Management is very worried *because* sales are falling.
2 After graduating, Miguel wanted to help his parents, ... he worked for a year in the sales department of their company.
3 Leila studied law at university, ... her dream was to find a job in marketing.
4 Our sales went up quickly .... our new products were very successful.
5 Piers was voted salesperson of the year .... he helped sales increase by 15%.
6 Tamara wanted to improve her English .... she decided to study for a diploma in business in Dublin.
7 Vladimir had a permanent position, ... he changed his job after a year .... he did not get on with his boss.

Editing

B Read the first part of a letter of reference.

- In most of the lines **1 – 8** there is **one extra word** which does not fit. Some lines, however, are correct.
- If a line is **correct**, put a tick (✔) in the space provided.
- If there is an **extra word** in the line, write that word in the space.

Dear Ms Eastwood

Thank you for your letter of the 2nd February about Marcel Lacour's　　1 ...✓......

an application for the job of Deputy Director.　　2 ..*an*.....

Marcel is worked with us for three years as Office Manager. Then he　　3 ....

worked for two years in the same position in the our Paris subsidiary.　　4 ....

He has a degree in Accountancy and Management, and he is currently　　5 ....

doing a part-time MBA. His knowledge of languages includes any　　6 ....

French, English, Greek and Polish. This makes him a very suitable　　7 ....

for work in a European of organisation.　　8 ....

C Now match these sentence halves to write the second part of the letter of reference.

1 He is an excellent manager, very dedicated to the staff
2 He is hard-working and gets
3 He motivates the staff and
4 He is good at dealing with problems and is very good at
5 Marcel is completely reliable and always
6 He has a very positive attitude to
7 I highly recommend him

a) is a good team leader.
b) for this post.
c) his work and is a creative and flexible person.
d) negotiating solutions.
e) meets his deadlines.
f) and to the quality of his work.
g) very good results.

Yours sincerely

Julian Ash
Director

Markets

Vocabulary

A Use the definitions to complete the puzzle and find the hidden adjective.

1 An ...... market is outside the producer's country.

2 An ...... market is good to enter.

3 The ...... market is the market in the producer's country.

4 A ...... market makes less and less money.

5 A ...... market does not grow much and does not have many competitors in it.

6 A ...... market is for a product that a lot of people buy.

7 A ...... market is the same as a large market.

8 A ...... market is for high quality and expensive goods.

9 A ...... market is small, but it very often makes money.

```
  ¹E  X  P  O  R  T
 ²A     [ ]  C
     ³H  [ ]
        F
⁴      C  [ ]
       ⁵     U
      ⁶   [ ]
       ⁷  [ ]
       ⁸     U
⁹    C  [ ]
```

Now complete the definition of the hidden word.

A .... market is one that makes money.

Vocabulary +

B Complete the text with the best words from page 33.

What is the secret of successful marketing?

The answer is easy: think about your ..9..1.

First, ...2 market research to get some information about the customers' needs. Then, supply exactly what the customers want. A successful product needs to be at the right ....3, and it needs to be ....4 at the right place. This means that you distribute it in the right way.

Finally, how do you want to present the product to customers? Think about ....5, image, advertising – in one word: promotion.

In ....6, just remember: Product, Price, Place, and Promotion. These are 'the four *Ps*' of the marketing mix. To market a ....7 successfully, you need to get this mix right.

1	**a)** customers	**b)** orders	**c)** sellers
2	**a)** do	**b)** make	**c)** work
3	**a)** expenses	**b)** cost	**c)** price
4	**a)** reliable	**b)** available	**c)** profitable
5	**a)** design	**b)** shop	**c)** type
6	**a)** end	**b)** conclusion	**c)** final
7	**a)** client	**b)** profit	**c)** product

Language review

Comparatives

A Write the missing letters to make the comparative form of ten adjectives.

1 small _er_
2 larg _ _
3 eas _ _ _
4 hot _ _ _
5 young _ _

6 new _ _
7 big _ _ _
8 happ _ _ _
9 earl _ _ _
10 quiet _ _

B Study these examples. Then match them to the spelling rules below.

Adjective	Comparative	Spelling rule
1 cheap	cheaper	_Rule e_
2 late	later	....
3 big	bigger	....
4 fast	faster	....
5 clean	cleaner	....
6 early	earlier	....

Spelling rules:

a) Adjectives ending in consonant + vowel + consonant: double the last consonant + -er.

b) Adjectives ending in consonant + y: change y to i + -er.

c) Adjectives ending in -e: + -r.

d) Adjectives ending in two consonants: + -er.

e) Adjectives ending in vowel + vowel + consonant: + -er.

C Complete the sentences with words from the box.

~~easiest~~ more   most   younger   worse   a   the   easier   than   difficult

1 I think the ..._easiest_... mobile to use is the Pronto-X.
2 Is South Korea a .... competitive market than Japan?
3 It is more .... to break into export markets than into home markets.
4 It's not just another good product – it's .... best product on the market.
5 Our customers are .... and richer than our competitors' customers.
6 Pete is one of the .... helpful colleagues I have.
7 Sales this month are a bit better .... they were last month.
8 Sales are not going up. We need to find .... better way of entering that market.
9 The design of this model is not very attractive, but it's .... to use than the RL202.
10 The rate of unemployment was .... last year than this year.

Language + **D** Study these sentences about large and small differences.

The Chinese market is	much a lot a little a bit	more attractive harder to break into	than the Ukrainian one.

Note

Much and *a little* are usually preferred in formal, written English.

Read the information about two mobile phones. Then match the sentence halves to describe the differences between them.

	Virga M100	Pronto-X
Price	€299.99	€149.99
Weight	120 grams	90 grams
Size	6 x 11 x 3 cm	6 x 10 x 2 cm
Special features	Has 20 ringtones Has built-in digital camera Comes with 3 fun games **Get €80 of free calls when you buy one!**	Has 5 ringtones Has built-in digital camera Comes with 10 fun games **Get €40 of free calls when you buy one!**

1 The Virga M100 is much
2 The Pronto-X is a lot
3 You get a lot more free calls
4 The Pronto-X is a bit smaller
5 The Virga M100 has a lot
6 The Virga M100 has a lot fewer
7 The Virga M100 is much

a) cheaper than the Virga M100.
b) than the Virga M100; it is only 6 x 10 x 2 cm.
c) heavier. It weighs 120 grams!
d) fun games than the Pronto-X
e) more expensive than the Pronto-X.
f) more ringtones than the Pronto-X.
g) when you buy a Virga M100.

E Read the information about a third mobile phone. Then complete the sentences.

	Star 8
Price	€90
Weight	85 grams
Size	6 x 10 x 2 cm
Special features	Has 2 ringtones **Get €10 of free calls when you buy one!**

1 The Star 8 is ...*a lot cheaper*...... than the Pronto-X.

2 The Pronto-X is .... heavier than the Star 8.

3 The Virga M100 is .... than the Star 8. It is 6 x 11 x 3 cm.

4 The Star 8 has .... ringtones than the Virga M100.

5 Both the Virga M100 and the Pronto-X are .... the Star 8, which costs only €90.

6 The Star 8 weighs only 85 grams. It is .... the Virga M100.

Writing
E-mails

A Complete the e-mail with phrases from the box.

~~for sending~~ like to know   look forward to   please confirm   interested in

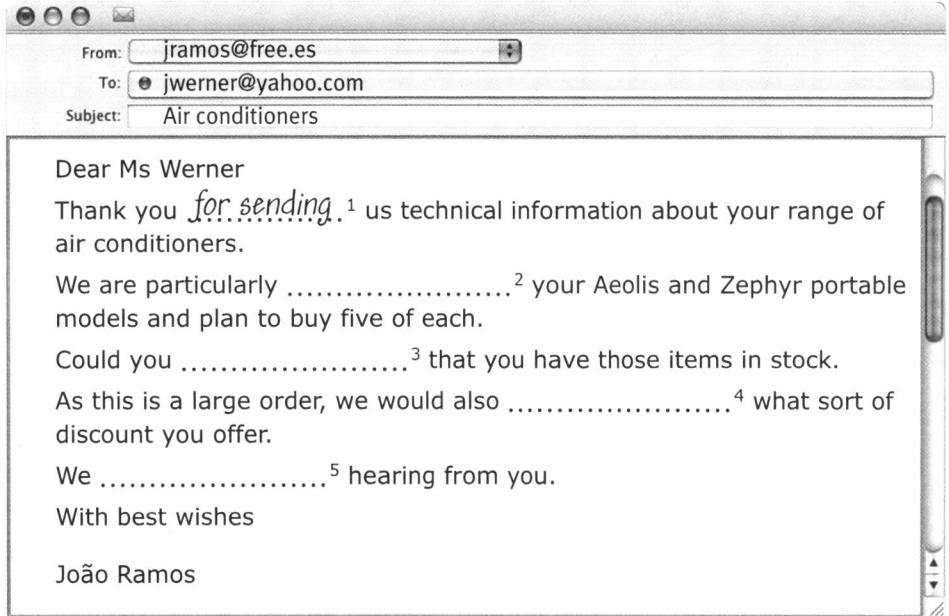

From: jramos@free.es
To: jwerner@yahoo.com
Subject: Air conditioners

Dear Ms Werner

Thank you *for sending*.¹ us technical information about your range of air conditioners.

We are particularly ....² your Aeolis and Zephyr portable models and plan to buy five of each.

Could you ....³ that you have those items in stock.

As this is a large order, we would also ....⁴ what sort of discount you offer.

We ....⁵ hearing from you.

With best wishes

João Ramos

Tip

In many e-mails and letters, information is often presented in the following order:

1 greeting
2 thanks / reference to earlier contact
3 most important point
4 other point(s)
5 reference to future contact
6 closing
7 signature

B Read the tip. Then put sentences a) to g) in the informal e-mail in the correct order, 1–7.

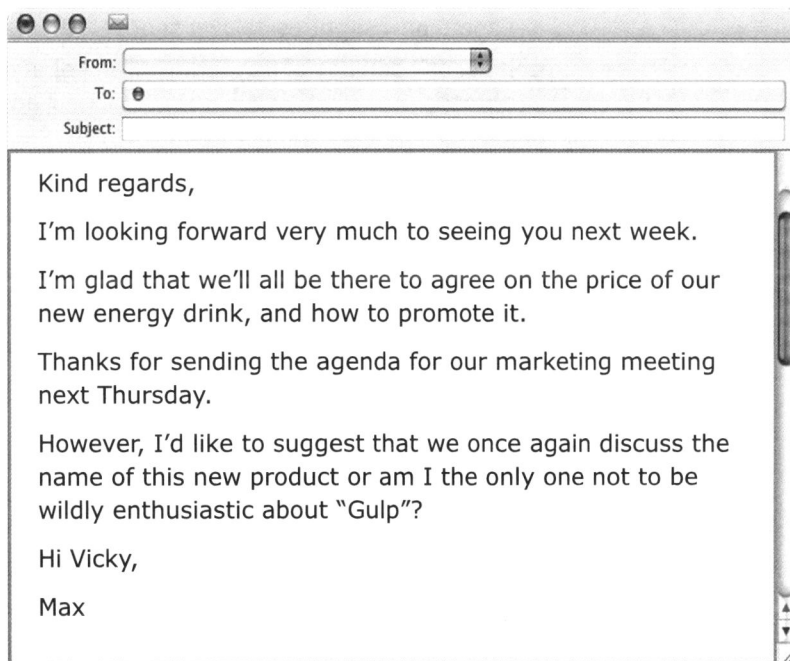

From:
To:
Subject:

a) | Kind regards, | ..6....
b) | I'm looking forward very much to seeing you next week. | ....
c) | I'm glad that we'll all be there to agree on the price of our new energy drink, and how to promote it. | ....
d) | Thanks for sending the agenda for our marketing meeting next Thursday. | ....
e) | However, I'd like to suggest that we once again discuss the name of this new product or am I the only one not to be wildly enthusiastic about "Gulp"? | ....
f) | Hi Vicky, | ....
g) | Max | ....

C Rewrite this e-mail using paragraphs, punctuation and capital letters where necessary.

hi tom mr stankov from impex contacted me this morning he is very unhappy because he hasnt received the samples of our new products he says he may not order from us again could you please send him another box of samples as soon as possible you know russia is a very important market for us and we dont want to lose this customer many thanks for dealing with this best regards kim

Hi Tom

Companies

Vocabulary

A **Complete the text with the correct form of verbs from the box.**

launch	have	~~begin~~	manufacture	provide	export

Sonara ..... *began* .....[1] in 1972 near Turin. Today, it ....[2] mainly aircraft engines, but in the 1970s it also ....[3] the car industry with components. It ....[4] a workforce of 2,000.

Sonara ....[5] 75% of its engines to other European countries. Last month, it ....[6] a new type of engine which burns 15% less fuel than other models.

B **Match the sentence halves.**

1 Panetti **employs** over 3,500 people,   **a)** but it plans to expand into France.

2 It **introduced** four new products last year,   **b)** including 1,400 in its own retail outlets.

3 It **makes** bread and   **c)** including sandwiches and pies.

4 Panetti only **supplies** its own shops;   **d)** many other bakery products.

5 It doesn't **sell** any of its products **abroad**,   **e)** it does not make products for anyone else.

C **Match these words and phrases from exercise A with a word or phrase from exercise B that has a similar meaning.**

1 manufactures = ... *makes* .....

2 provided = ...

3 has a workforce of = ...

4 export = ...

5 launched = ...

Notes

Make and *manufacture* do not have exactly the same meaning. To *manufacture* means to 'make large quantities of goods in a factory, using machines'. You *manufacture* (or *make*) cars, drugs, plastic goods, etc, but you usually *make* (not *manufacture*) bread, cheese, etc.

D **Complete each sentence with a phrase from the box.**

> **a)** about future projects.
> **b)** for quality control.
> **c)** in international construction projects.
> **d)** a new product.
> **e)** ~~of a department of 15 staff.~~
> **f)** under the brand name *Tekko*.

1 Juliette is in charge ..*e*..

2 Panetti is going to create .....

3 Alex is responsible .....

4 They manufacture plastic furniture .....

5 Jo and Francis are involved .....

6 She likes to make presentations .....

Language review

Present continuous

A Study these spelling rules for the *-ing* form.

Spelling rules	Infinitive	*-ing* form
Most verbs just add *-ing*.	market go	marketing going
If the verb ends in *e*, take away *e* and add *-ing*.	improve save	improving saving
If the verb ends in consonant + vowel + consonant, double the final consonant and add *-ing*;	set up transfer	setting up transferring
but do **not** double the final consonant if it is in an unstressed syllable.	deliver target	delivering targeting

B Write the *-ing* form of these verbs.

1 stay .*staying*....
2 listen ....
3 increase ....
4 develop ....
5 take ....

6 run ....
7 refer ....
8 work ....
9 try ....
10 deal ....

C Write the missing word in each of the following sentences.

1 I *am* translating our company's mission statement into Korean.
2 Many foreign companies investing in Turkey.
3 Sonara's sales figures improving?
4 I looking for a manager with a lot of experience in finance.
5 Tom still checking the company accounts?
6 Unfortunately, the east of the country not attracting many investors.
7 You planning to break into the Spanish market, aren't you?

D Write short answers to these questions.

1 Is the situation getting better?
Yes, ..*it is*.......... .
2 Are Sonara and Alfitel working together now?
Yes, ...
3 Are they improving the quality of their services?
No, ...
4 Is Mr Robertson looking for a bigger factory?
No, ...
5 Are you and Robert testing our new product?
Yes, ...
6 Hi Sam! So you aren't working for RTS Sports any more?
No, ...
7 Is Barbara trying to get money for her new project?
Yes, ...
8 Is their new shop attracting a lot of customers?
No, ...

E Complete these sentences with either the present simple or the present continuous form of the verbs in brackets.

1 We _develop_ three or four new products every year.
   Currently, we _are developing_ a new type of air conditioner. (develop)

2 I think our sales figures .... this May. This is unexpected – normally they .... in autumn and winter. (improve)

3 It generally .... only one year to develop a new product, but the FX200 .... longer because of technical problems. (take)

4 Mrs Wu .... all our product presentations. This week, she .... our next presentation in Vancouver. (organise)

5 This is where we .... our products. As you can see, Martin .... some cosmetics from our latest range. (test)

6 We .... Sonara's laboratory until our new one is ready. Otherwise, we never .... other people's facilities. (use)

Language +

F Complete the sentences with the correct form (present simple or present continuous) of the verbs from the box. Use each verb twice.

| translate | employ | speak | think | answer |

1 Ana _is translating_ this year's directors' report into Russian.

2 Bertrand .... the phone this week because our secretary is away.

3 How many people .... the company .... ?

4 Can you hold? Mr Souayah .... on the other line.

5 Business is so good that we .... an extra 200 staff.

6 Our manager .... we should open a new subsidiary in France.

7 They .... of expanding into the new markets of Central Asia.

8 We .... all our customers' calls politely and efficiently.

9 We always .... all our company brochures into five languages.

10 I think I can get a very good job in Asia because I .... Chinese.

Writing Editing

A Read this information about Shanghai Tang, the Chinese clothes design company.

- In most of the lines **1–10** there is **one wrong word**. Some lines, however, are correct.
- If a line is **correct**, put a tick (✓) in the space provided.
- If there is a wrong word in the line, **underline the wrong word** in the text and **write the correct word** in the space.

Shanghai Tang manufactures and selling designer clothes and fashion accessories 1 _sells_

inspired by traditional Chinese culture. The brand's founder, David Tang, is from 2 ✓

Hong Kong. 'We make traditional Chinese clothes and we modernise them,' she says. 3 ....

Joanne Ooi, the company's creative director, does a lot of research when she plan a 4 ....

new collection. Her designers made clothes that are luxurious and elegant, but 5 ....

they are clothes that people want to wearing because they make them feel special. 6 ....

Shanghai Tang grew 40% in 2005. Its parent company is the Richemont Luxury 7 ....

Group, which also owns Cartier, Montblanc, Chloé and several other global brand. 8 ....

Shanghai Tang has its flagship store in Hong Kong's Central District, and its also 9 ....

has 20 store in cities like Paris, Tokyo, London, New York and Zurich. 10 ....

Richemont is now developing an ambitious plan: to launch five stores a year in the

world's most dynamic markets.

B Rewrite this letter using paragraphs, punctuation and capital letters where necessary.

dear sir or madam we are writing to request further information about your new range of trainers we are a large chain of retailers of sportswear we are looking for a manufacturer of footwear for the french market we operate from over 400 stores and always order in large quantities could you please send us details of special discounts for such orders and your latest catalogue we look forward to hearing from you yours faithfully barbara costa

Dear Sir or Madam

We are ...

Company literature

C Complete the text with words or phrases from the box.

not only	but also	The first one
The second one	Finally	For example
	as well as	

WELCOME TO

R F C GROUP

RFC Group plc is one of the largest financial services companies in the country. It has branches ...*not only*......[1] in the capital, ...[2] in four other cities.

RFC is rapidly expanding overseas. ....[3], it already has operations in Brazil, Poland and Turkey.

RFC has two main divisions. ....[4] is its Financial Services Division. This division provides independent financial advice to start-up companies.

..................[5], the Internet Technology Division, provides secure e-mail services ....[6] access to online databases.

..................[7], it also has a unit helping small companies design their own web pages.

The Web

Language work

Vocabulary

A **Use the clues to complete the crossword puzzle.**

Across

1 More and more retailers . . . . . their products on the Internet. (4)

2 andrea@skynet.be This is how you read this e-mail address: "andrea at skynet . . . . . b e". (3)

4 We always book our concert tickets . . . . . ., so we don't have to queue. (6)

7 If the bank . . . . . . your account, it pays money into it. (7)

8 . . . . . . is great to keep in touch with family and friends, and it's cheaper than the phone. (5)

9 If you . . . . . . your credit card details, you enter them. (3)

Down

1 This diagram . . . . . . you how an Internet transaction is made. (5)

2 If the bank . . . . . . your account, it takes money out of it. (6)

3 Their . . . . . . address is http://www.fashion1.ie (7)

5 If a seller . . . . . . an order, he or she carries it out. (7)

6 When you send your credit card details, there is a system to . . . . . . all the information immediately. (6)

7 To send the message, just . . . . . . on the 'send' button. (5)

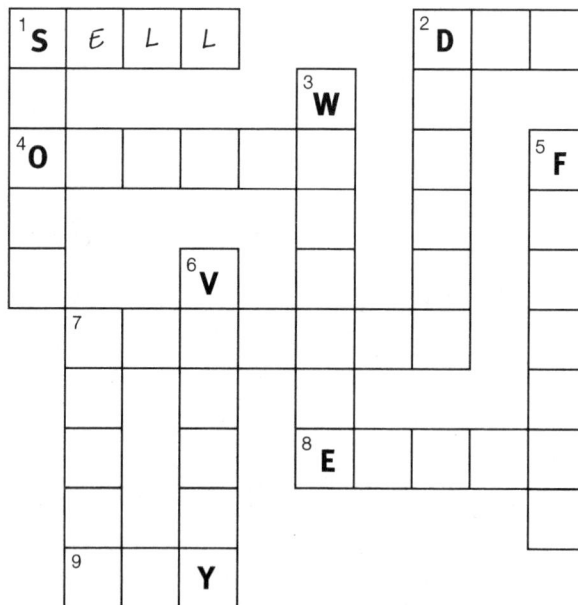

B **Complete each sentence with a word from the box.**

crash   download   ~~log on~~   search engine   virus

1 To ..*log on*.., just type in your username and password.

2 When computer systems . . . ., people can lose a lot of files.

3 I often use Google. I think it's a very good . . . .

4 You can . . . . our annual report in PDF format.

5 Be careful when you download files. Sometimes they have a . . . .

Prepositions

C Complete the e-mail with suitable prepositions.

From: Tim
To: Alex
Subject: Brussels trip

Alex,

Here is your draft programme.

You are leaving ..*on*...¹ Saturday, 7 June ....² 10:45 from Dublin Airport, arriving at Brussels S. Charleroi at 1:15. That's local time, so don't worry! You're flying Ryanair, flight number FR44.

The company driver will be ....³ the airport to meet you and take you ....⁴ your hotel ....⁵ the centre of Brussels. ....⁶ the Métropole Hotel, it is just a three-minutes' walk ....⁷ the Chamber of Commerce.

Sunday is a free day, but Mr Vermeulen will probably take you ....⁸ for dinner. He too likes to be well-prepared ....⁹ meetings!

The meetings ....¹⁰ Monday start at 8:30 ....¹¹ the morning and will probably go on ....¹² lunchtime, which is 12:15. Lunch is at the Métropole.

At 1:30, Mr Vermeulen is taking you to the 'E-commerce for Europe' event. The driver will then take you ....¹³ the airport in plenty of time ....¹⁴ flight FR47, departing 6:40 and arriving ....¹⁵ Dublin 7:10.

Please confirm ....¹⁶ the end of the week that these arrangements are OK.

Tim

Language review

Future forms

A Complete the sentences with a form of *be going to* and a verb from the box.

    ~~study~~   expand   meet   call   put   talk

1 Mark doesn't want to go on the computer skills course now.
   He's going to study...... accountancy instead.
2 I don't want to send the contract as an e-mail attachment.
   .... it in the post.
3 Business is good. We .... into Central Asia.
4 A: The title of his presentation is *Get Online*!
   B: .... he .... about the benefits of e-commerce again?
5 The sales figures are good, and I can see that the department .... its target this month.
6 Sandra has the phone numbers of over 100 customers. .... them one by one for the marketing survey.

B Match the sentence halves to make predictions.

1 I'm sure the volume of e-commerce will
2 Call her at 3:30 –
3 We won't have enough money to
4 I think there will be
5 The figures so far aren't very good, so we won't
6 The system has to be more secure,

a) more control over the Internet.
b) or people won't shop online.
c) increase in the next five years.
d) meet our target.
e) she'll be in her office then.
f) change all our computers.

Language work

C **Complete the sentences with *'ll, will* or *won't*.**

1 Anna doesn't like her new boss. She thinks she *'ll*..... change her job soon.

2 I .... have time to go to the trade fair, I'm afraid. There's far too much work at the office!

3 Try to meet your sales target, so you .... get a bonus at the end of the year.

4 Next year .... be our 10th anniversary.

5 Liz hasn't got enough information, so she .... be able to finish her report on time.

6 Many people .... shop online because they're worried about security.

7 We checked everything carefully. There .... be any problems this time.

8 Think about how customers .... use your website.

9 I can see you're very busy. Don't worry, I .... do it for you.

10 In a few years' time, everyone .... have broadband Internet access.

D **Write one word in each sentence to make correct future forms.**

1 They going to redesign their website.

They're going to redesign their website.

2 'My computer's not working properly.' 'Don't worry. I call our IT specialist.'

3 Our visitors from Korea arriving next Thursday at 11:30.

4 We can't be sure that people have more free time in 20 years' time.

5 Are you going apply for the post of Systems Analyst with Crawley Electronics?

6 Do you think you be able to come to the conference?

7 I can't make it tomorrow morning, I'm afraid. I giving a talk at the trade fair.

8 It cost too much to employ an extra IT assistant.

9 We are certain Internet security going to get better.

10 I have the report on your desk before Friday. I promise.

Writing

Word order

A **Put the words in the correct order to make sentences.**

1 Dave / I think / take / the 9:45 plane / to Glasgow. / will

I think Dave will take the 9:45 plane to Glasgow.

2 catch / earlier / flight. / He / the / won't

3 8:45. / check / won't / He / in / until

4 He / a / be / hopes / there / won't / delay.

5 Judith / a / book / him / on / will / later flight.

6 She / book / him / early morning / on / the / won't / flight.

7 arrives / at 10:50, / Dave / for the meeting. / he / so / late / won't be

B **Match the sentence halves to make some predictions about the future.**

1 Everybody will

2 Businesses won't be

3 More and more people will

4 Internet security won't

5 High street banks won't

6 All companies will

a) have a website for their customers and their staff.

b) do their shopping online.

c) disappear, but many people will prefer online banking.

d) able to compete without an online operation.

e) be able to access the Internet from their mobile phones.

f) be a problem any more.

E-mails

C **Complete these e-mails with words or phrases from the box.**

> arriving   delay   early   I should   later   leaving   Please   Sorry
>
> ~~Thanks~~   you'll

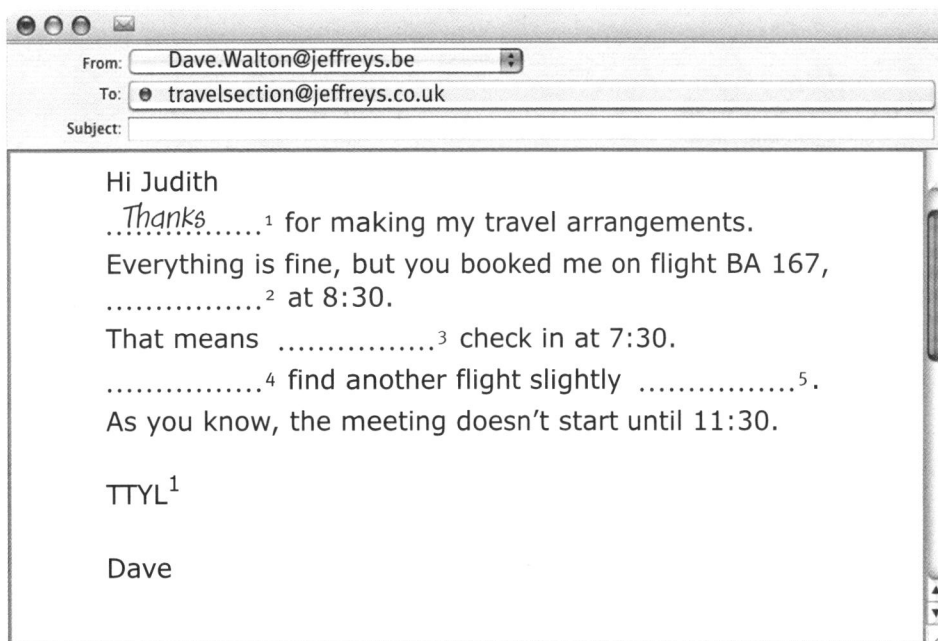

From: Dave.Walton@jeffreys.be
To: travelsection@jeffreys.co.uk
Subject:

Hi Judith

..._Thanks_.....¹ for making my travel arrangements.

Everything is fine, but you booked me on flight BA 167, ...² at 8:30.

That means ....³ check in at 7:30.

...............⁴ find another flight slightly ....⁵.

As you know, the meeting doesn't start until 11:30.

TTYL¹

Dave

¹ Text abbreviation for 'talk to you later'.

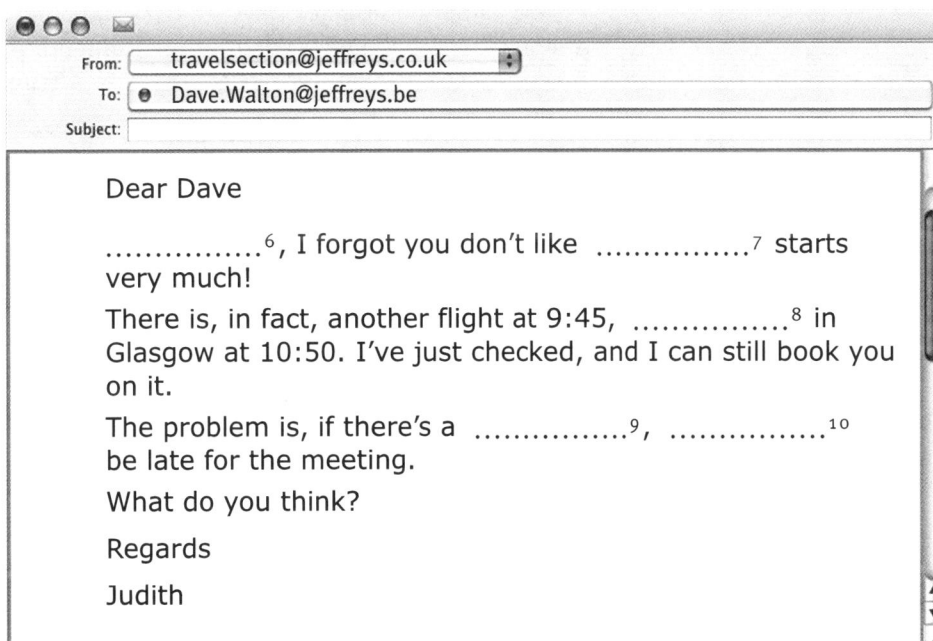

From: travelsection@jeffreys.co.uk
To: Dave.Walton@jeffreys.be
Subject:

Dear Dave

...............⁶, I forgot you don't like ....⁷ starts very much!

There is, in fact, another flight at 9:45, ...⁸ in Glasgow at 10:50. I've just checked, and I can still book you on it.

The problem is, if there's a ....⁹, ...¹⁰ be late for the meeting.

What do you think?

Regards

Judith

D **Write Dave's reply to Judith.**

- Confirm which flight you want.
- Say <u>why</u> you want either the 8.30 or the 9.45 flight.

Hi Judith,

Cultures

Language work

Vocabulary

A **Complete the text with the best words.**

When people hear the word *culture*, they often think about the cultural life, the history or the ....*a*....[1] of a country. But when you are in business, you also need to think about *company cultures*.

Companies have different *cultures*: they believe in different things, and they have different ways of working.

For example, some companies are formal, so staff use ......[2] when they speak to each other, and they have to wear business ......[3]. Other companies have a system of ......[4] Fridays, when staff can ......[5] anything they like at the end of the week.

Sometimes, there are also big differences in the amount of time ......[6] that staff can get. In some companies, staff get more paid annual ......[7] than in others, for example. Or staff can choose when they start and finish work – a system called '......'[8]. People can start work at 8, 9 or 10 a.m. and finish at 4, 5 or 6 p.m.

Finally, bosses and employees can communicate in many different ways. Some line managers like to get regular written reports, but others prefer ......[9] communication.

1 **a)** customs	**b)** uses	**c)** habits
2 **a)** family names	**b)** positions	**c)** business cards
3 **a)** dressing	**b)** fashion	**c)** suits
4 **a)** formal	**b)** casual	**c)** normal
5 **a)** wear	**b)** suit	**c)** dress
6 **a)** out	**b)** off	**c)** away
7 **a)** weekends	**b)** benefit	**c)** leave
8 **a)** shift work	**b)** part time	**c)** flexitime
9 **a)** back-to-front	**b)** face-to-face	**c)** back-to-back

Vocabulary +

B **Study the patterns to make new words and expand your vocabulary.**

Noun		Adjective
culture	→	cultural
politics	→	political
logic	→	..............[1]
mathematics	→	..............[2]
nature	→	..............[3]
economy	→	economic / economical
history	→	..............[4] / ....[5]

Now study the examples and definitions on page 45.

Examples

We will solve our country's **economic** problems.

We are looking for a more **economical** way of heating our offices.

The Queen's visit was a **historic** occasion for our country.

My new colleague likes **historical** novels about 18th-century Italy.

Definitions

Economic means 'connected with the trade and industry of a country, or with the money that a society has'.

Economical means 'using money or time without wasting it'.

Historic means 'important in history; something people will always remember'.

Historical means 'connected with the past or with the study of history'.

C Complete the sentences with words from exercise B.

1 Our organisation now has a modern, business-like management cul.*ture*. .

2 Investors were very worried because of the pol......... problems in the region.

3 The two leaders discussed eco......... cooperation between their countries.

4 We make all our Avalon skin-care products from nat......... ingredients.

5 Our city is not only a business centre, it also has a lot of cul......... events.

6 India is a fast-growing eco......... .

7 Don't talk about pol......... or religion. These are taboo topics here.

8 We all know that the car is not the most eco............... form of transport.

Language review

should / shouldn't

A Match each item on the left with a sentence on the right.

1 Do you think I should buy my hosts a present?

2 He should try to be a bit more punctual.

3 I don't think you should wear formal clothes to the party.

4 I think someone should talk to the boss.

5 She should go on the training course, too.

6 You shouldn't miss any of the meetings.

a) I think all our staff need to develop their computer skills.

b) Most of the guests will be in jeans.

c) People in this country think it's rude to be late.

d) They are always very kind to me.

e) They're always very useful.

f) We can't work extra hours on Saturday!

B Complete the sentences with *should* or *shouldn't*.

1 We .*should*...... order online. It's faster.

2 We .... be late for meetings. It's rude.

3 You .... say anything about the food.

4 I don't think you .... interrupt the presenter. She'll take questions at the end.

5 I think Sandra .... move to another department. She's not happy in Sales.

6 They .... use children in advertisements. I find it shocking.

7 Do you think I .... apologise for this short delay?

8 I don't think you .... use first names. They have a rather formal company culture.

C Complete the text with *should* or *shouldn't*.

Doing business in Japan

People planning to do business in Japan *should*.1 know a few things about the country, its tradition and its people.

First of all, you ....2 hire a good interpreter – someone who speaks the language and who knows the customs and traditions.

Many people in Japan shake hands when they meet, but you ....3 be too fast. You ....4 wait and see if they offer their hand first.

When somebody gives you their business card, you ....5 look at it and read it carefully. You ....6 write on it, because Japanese people think this is very impolite.

Some advice about meetings – you ....7 worry about silences during a meeting. You ....8 respect those silences. And finally, remember that you ....9 make too much eye contact.

could / would **D** A business person is entertaining a colleague at home. Complete these conversation extracts with *Could I / Could you* or *Would you.*

1 A: This chocolate mousse is delicious. *Could I* .... have some more?

B: Of course! We made it especially for you.

2 B: .... like a cigarette?

A: No, thanks. I don't smoke any longer.

3 A: That was a lovely meal. Thank you very much.

B: .... like tea or coffee?

4 A: .... make a quick phone call, please? My mobile is at home.

B: Sure! Use the phone in the study. It's quieter in there.

5 A: Now then, about that meeting I missed this morning. .... tell me what it was about?

B: Well, we just discussed the details of the product launch.

6 A: .... order me a taxi, please? It's getting late.

B: .... like a lift to the station?

Writing

Linkers

A Complete the sentences with the correct linker from the box.

| and (x2)   because (x2)   but (x2)   so (x2) |

1 Before I left for South Korea, I learnt to speak a little of the local language ....*and*.... read about the history of the country.

2 We wear formal clothes, ... we always use first names when we speak to each other.

3 I felt uncomfortable .... there was a long silence during the meal.

4 Their employees aren't happy about the changes, ... many of them are leaving.

5 Our new boss is OK, ... we don't likethe changes he wants to make.

6 The new manager is having a difficult time .... he doesn't understand local culture.

7 I had a lot of training in cross-cultural relations, ... I feel prepared to work abroad.

8 In my last job it was more relaxed. People used first names, ... there was no dress code.

B You are an employee in a company where many things are changing. You are not happy about some of the changes.
Write an e-mail to the human resources manager. Explain what you are unhappy about and ask for an appointment to see her.

Organise your e-mail like this:

1 Start with *Dear Ms Roberts*.

2 Say one or two positive things about your job and/or the company.

3 Briefly explain your problems (choose two or three points from the list, or use your imagination).

4 Ask when Ms Roberts could see you to talk about this in more detail.

5 Close with a suitable ending.

Problems

- you have to wear a uniform at all times
- not enough face-to-face communication
- too many meetings
- fixed working hours
- a lot of paperwork

Topic sentences

C Match the sentence halves.

1 Food is important
2 In my country, most people live
3 Most people have small families –
4 Visitors often say
5 School starts early – seven o'clock! –

a) and most people start work at that time too.
b) for both young and old people.
c) in flats, not houses.
d) usually one or two children.
e) that we are hospitable.

These sentences are used to begin the five paragraphs in exercise D. They tell us something about the topic of each paragraph. That is why they are sometimes called *topic sentences*.

D Choose the correct topic sentences from exercise C for these paragraphs.

a) ....2.... However, many people have a small house in the country. They like to spend their weekends there.

b) .... Only ten years ago, the average was four children. The situation is different now, partly because both men and women want a career.

c) .... We also finish early, and that is good. School is over at 1:30, and a lot of office workers finish at 2:00.

d) .... Many people are happy with just a snack before school or work, but dinner is a special occasion for everyone, every day. It is usually at about seven o'clock in the evening. We don't eat fast, so dinner sometimes goes on until after eight.

e) .... We like meeting new people. We are a small country, so we have to be open to the world. Also, tourism is one of our main industries.

Language work

A **Complete the job advertisements with the best words.**

Sales/Account Manager
Salary: £24,000 per year
Edinburgh-based company is seeking a person with sales experience to ..*d*..¹ sales worldwide and to .....² a large department in the clothing industry.

The person will also need to .....³ communication between our production, sales and marketing departments.

Background in clothing manufacturing essential.

Please contact: Sarah Atkinson atkinson@btinternet.com or Fax: 0131 123 7650.

Telesales Executive
Salary: £20,000 per year
Our Telesales Executive will have the .....⁴ to make effective phone calls to marketing contacts and to .....⁵ business meetings for our clients.

Bebop offers excellent training and promotion .....⁶.

Call Paul Glover on 020 4456 1090 or e-mail: beboprecruit@easynet.co.uk

Sales Manager
Salary: £26,000 per year
Conference and Events Company urgently requires a Sales Manager to .....⁷ a team of 8 telesales executives.

You will .....⁸ the team and .....⁹ all sales staff and their problems. In addition, you will .....¹⁰ future marketing campaigns and .....¹¹ a new marketing strategy.

Background of the candidate: experience in telesales and direct sales; at least 3 years' management experience.

Location: Cheshire

Contact: Karen Poulson, tel. 01260 271288, e-mail: cec@events.co.uk

1 a) increase	**b)** set up	**c)** lead
2 a) manage	**b)** train	**c)** direct
3 a) create	**b)** plan	**c)** improve
4 a) interest	**b)** ability	**c)** responsibility
5 a) work	**b)** organise	**c)** communicate
6 a) opportunities	**b)** facilities	**c)** qualities
7 a) boss	**b)** lead	**c)** drive
8 a) apply	**b)** practise	**c)** train
9 a) set up	**b)** deal with	**c)** look for
10 a) train	**b)** control	**c)** plan
11 a) improve	**b)** develop	**c)** increase

B **Study the examples and the tip, and complete the sentences. Use *for*, *as* or *in*.**
Examples:

Stephen works **for** an engineering company.

Gerhard works **as** a receptionist.

Sandra works **in** education.

Isabelle works **in** a French restaurant.

Tip

- Use *work for* when you talk about the company or organisation where someone is employed.
- Use *work as* + job.
- Use *work in* + kind of activity.
- Also, use *work in* with words like bank, hotel, hospital or factory.

1 He has worked ...*as*... an air traffic controller.
2 Have you worked .... the food industry?
3 At the moment, he is working .... a travel agency.
4 Would you like to work .... mechanical engineering?
5 Sandra's husband works .... the BBC.
6 Are you going to work .... a clothing company in Edinburgh?
7 Rachel is going to work .... a consultant for a design company.

Language review

Present perfect

A **Put the verbs in brackets in the present perfect.**

1 ...*Have*.. you ..*known*.. each other for a long time? (*know*)
2 .... Pierre and Lucien .... jobs frequently? (*change*)
3 .... Anna .... several jobs since leaving university? (*have*)
4 .... Laura and Stella both .... for the same job? (*apply*)
5 .... you and Tim ever .... difficulties getting along with Mr Dumas? (*have*)
6 .... you ever .... in Central Asia? (*work*)

B **Match these answers to the questions in exercise A.**

a) Pierre hasn't. But Lucien has had three or four different ones already. ☐ 2
b) No, we haven't. We met at a conference only last week, in fact. ☐
c) Yes, I have. I worked in Kazakhstan from 1998 to 2001. ☐
d) Yes, she has. I don't know how many, though. ☐
e) Yes, they have. That's a coincidence, isn't it? ☐
f) Yes, we have. Especially me. ☐

C **Complete the short answers with the correct form of *have*.**

1 A: Has François ever worked in a bank?
  B: No, ..*he hasn't*........
2 A: Have all the candidates for interview arrived?
  B: Yes, ...
3 A: So you have worked for Nielsen Electronics, is that right?
  B: Yes, ...
4 A: What about these candidates? Have they ever managed a project?
  B: No, ...
5 A: Have you called a job agency?
  B: No, ...
6 A: Have you and Luis received a reply yet?
  B: Well, Luis .... , but I'm afraid I ....

D Complete the two sentences with the correct time expressions from the box. There are several possible expressions for each sentence.

1 three months ago	**6** yesterday morning
2 this year	**7** so far
3 for the past ten days	**8** over the last five years
4 last week	**9** in 2007
5 at 9 o'clock	**10** five minutes ago

a) The last time I saw her was ..1. 4.......

b) They haven't been very successful ....

E Complete the telephone conversation with the items in brackets. Use the present perfect or the simple past.

Rose: Hi, Michelle. I'm calling about our advert for the post of personal assistant. ..*Has anybody expressed*. (*anybody / express*)1 any interest yet?

Michelle: Yes, it's all going very well. We .... (*receive*)2 thirty-one applications so far. And yesterday alone about ten people .... (*phone*)3 for further details of the job.

Rose: Excellent. So how many applicants .... (*you / select*)4?

Michelle: Well, I .... (*start*)5 working on the selection as soon as I .... (*arrive*)6 this morning. I'm afraid I .... (*not / finish*)7 yet, but I .... (*already / select*)8 eight candidates, all with the right qualifications and experience.

Rose: Very good. .... (*you / invite*)9 them for interview yet?

Michelle: Well, no. I .... (*think*)10 you'd like to have a look at all the applications yourself first.

Rose: I won't be back in the office till Friday, I'm afraid, so just go ahead, Michelle. You know I trust you 200%!

Michelle: Thanks. OK then. I'll finish selecting candidates and invite them for interview as soon as I .... (*finish*)11 the conference programme. I .... (*not / have*)12 time to deal with it yesterday, with all those phone calls.

Writing

Word order

A Put the words in the interview questions in the correct order.

1 What / got / skills / you / have / ?   *What skills have you got?*
2 What / strengths / your / are / ?
3 What / time / do / do / free / in / your / you / ?
4 What / work / people / you / of / with / kind / do / well / ?
5 What / greatest / been / achievement / your / has / ?
6 What / job / like / about / did / last / you / your / ?
7 What / in / do / do / to / future / you / the / want / ?

B Answer the questions in exercise A. Use your imagination if you wish.

Job applications

C When people apply for a job, they usually send a covering letter together with their CV. In this letter, they give further information to explain why they think they are suitable for the job. Carol Avery is applying for the post of Sales Manager (see page 48). Complete Carol's covering letter (sent as an e-mail) with items from the box.

> **a)** As you will see from my CV,
>
> **b)** I am very interested in the post you are offering
>
> **c)** I look forward to hearing
>
> **d)** ~~I would like to apply for the position~~
>
> **e)** In addition,
>
> **f)** Please let me know
>
> **g)** When I was with Melrose Computers,

Language work

From: avery@durham.co.uk

To: cec@events.co.uk

Subject: Covering letter

Dear Ms Poulson

...*d*...1 of Sales Manager advertised in *The Chester Telegraph* on 7 September.

........2 I have worked as Assistant Human Resources Manager for four years. I am responsible for training for new staff, and also for organising problem-solving courses for senior staff.

........3 I have managed a number of projects for our overseas subsidiaries. This included a training project for local sales staff in Hong Kong.

........4 I also gained a lot of experience in telesales and direct sales.

........5 because I would like to be involved in both telesales and direct sales. I would also like to use my skills as a trainer in a more challenging environment.

........6 if there are any other details you need.

........7 from you.

Yours sincerely

Carol Avery

Talk business

Introduction

The aim of this *Talk business* section is to make you more aware of some of the main features of English pronunciation. This will help you understand spoken English more easily. It can also help you discover areas you may need to work on for your spoken English to sound more natural.

The sounds of English

🎧 **Look, listen and repeat.**

Vowel sounds

/ɪ/	quick fix	/ɔː/	short course
/iː/	clean sheet	/ʊ/	good books
/e/	sell well	/uː/	school rules
/æ/	bad bank	/ʌ/	much luck
/ɑː/	smart card	/ɜː/	first term
/ɒ/	top job	/ə/	a'bout 'Canada

Diphthongs

/eɪ/	play safe	/əʊ/	go slow
/aɪ/	my price	/ɪə/	near here
/ɔɪ/	choice oil	/eə/	fair share
/aʊ/	downtown	/ʊə/	tour

Consonants

1 Contrasting voiceless and voiced consonants

Voiceless		Voiced	
/p/	pay	/b/	buy
/f/	file	/v/	value
/t/	tax	/d/	deal
/θ/	think	/ð/	this
/tʃ/	cheap	/dʒ/	job
/s/	sell	/z/	zero
/k/	card	/g/	gain
/ʃ/	option	/ʒ/	decision

2 Other consonants

/m/	mine	/l/	loss	/n/	net	/r/	rise
/ŋ/	branding	/w/	win	/h/	high	/j/	year

> **Tips**
>
> - Find out which sounds you have difficulty recognising or producing and focus mainly on these.
> - Add your own key words in the Sounds of English section for the sounds you wish to focus on.
> - Use the pause button on your cassette or CD player. This will give you time to speak or write when you do the exercises.

Using a dictionary

Any good dictionary today gives you useful information on the pronunciation of individual words. With the help of the *Longman Business English Dictionary* or the *Longman Wordwise Dictionary*, for example, you will be able to work out the pronunciation of any English word on your own, once you are familiar with the phonemic symbols.

In addition, a dictionary also gives you essential information about *word stress*. When a word has more than one syllable, we always put more stress on one of the syllables, that is, we say that syllable more strongly. Look at the dictionary entry for *compete*:

> **com•pete** /kəmˈpiːt/ v [I] to try to win something or to be more successful than someone else:

The sign ' shows you that the syllable immediately after it should be stressed: comPETE.

You will find various exercises on word stress in units 1, 5, 6, 8 and 11.

What about the sign ːʔ The sign ː shows you that the vowel is long. The contrast between *long* and *short* vowels is very important for people to understand each other. In unit 5, for example, you will find an exercise on /ɪ/ and /iː/, and unit 12 has an exercise on /ɒ/ and /ɔː/.

Sounds and spelling

In English, (a) you can spell the same sound in different ways, or (b) you can pronounce the same letters in different ways.

(a) Consider for example /əʊ/, the sound of *go slow*. You can spell it *o* as in *open*, *oa* as in *loan*, *oe* as in *toe*, *ough* as in *although*, *ow* as in *know*, or *eou* as in *Seoul*.

(b) Take the letter *u*, for instance. You pronounce it /ʌ/ as in *cut*, /ʊ/ as in *full*, /ɜː/ as in *turn*, /ɔː/ as in *sure*, /uː/ as in *tune*, or /ɪ/ as in *busy*.

Put the following words under the correct sound in the table below (the letters in bold show the sound).

break	conscious	heart	knowledge	advice
their	buyer	Europe	height	laugh
said	train	chair	friendship	insurance
million		scientific		want

Vowels

/ɒ/	/e/	/ɑː/
1 job	1 sell	1 card
2	2	2 ....
3	3	3 ....

/ eɪ/	/eə/	/aɪ/
1 pay	1 share	1 price
2	2	2 ....
3	3	3 ....

Consonants

/ʃ/	/s/	/j/
1 option	1 sell	1 year
2	2	2 ....
3	3	3 ....

There are exercises about a variety of sound–spelling relationships in units 1, 2, 3, 4, 5 and 6.

Shadowing

Shadowing is a very effective way to make the most of the recorded material.

1 Play a short section – a few words or one line of a dialogue – and then pause.

2 Without speaking, repeat internally what you heard.

3 Play the same section again. Pause and speak the words in exactly the same way and at the same speed. Repeat this step until you are completely satisfied with your performance.

4 Play the same section again and speak along with the voice on the recording. This is shadowing.

5 Move on to the next short section of the recording and repeat the same procedure.

UNIT 1　Introductions

Individual sounds

A 🎧 **1.1 Listen to how the letters in bold are pronounced in the following words. Do they sound the same (✔) or different (✗)?**

1	German	Turkish	✔	5 Russian	Kuwaiti
2	France	Japan	✗	6 England	Italy
3	Poland	Oman		7 Brazilian	American
4	Swedish	Greek			

🎧 **1.1 Check your answers. Then listen again and practise saying the words.**

B 🎧 **1.2 Listen to these words. Notice the sound changes.**

France　　　French
/ɑː/　　　　/e/

Spain　　　Spanish
/eɪ/　　　　/æ/

Denmark　　Danish
/e/　　　　 /eɪ/

Wales　　　Welsh
/eɪ/　　　　/e/

🎧 **1.2 Listen again and practise saying the words.**

Connected speech

C 🎧 **1.3 Listen to the way certain words can be linked.**

an‿engineer　　She's‿an‿engineer.
a sales‿assistant　　He's‿a sales‿assistant‿in‿a supermarket.

D 🎧 **1.4 Listen to these sentences and show the links that you hear.**

1 Peter is an accountant in Aachen.

2 Azim is an Uzbek airline pilot.

3 This is Olga. She works in Omsk.

4 Tim, meet Alan. He's in Accounts.

5 Liz works as a chemist for an Irish company.

🎧 **1.4 Check your answers. Then listen again, and practise the sentences.**

Stress and intonation

E 🎧 **1.5 Listen to these words. Notice the stressed syllables (see Introduction, pages 52 and 53).**

Bra.<u>zil</u>　　Bra.<u>zil</u>.ian　　*The stress is on <u>the same</u> syllable.*
<u>Chi</u>.na　　Chi.<u>nese</u>　　*The stress is on <u>a different</u> syllable.*

F 🎧 **1.6 Listen to the recording and underline the stressed syllables, as in exercise E.**

1 She's from A.mer.i.ca　　　She's A.mer.i.can

2 He's from It.al.y　　　　　He's I.tal.ian

3 They're from Brit.ain　　　They're Brit.ish

4 I'm from Ja.pan　　　　　I'm Jap.a.nese

5 We're from Can.a.da　　　We're Ca.na.di.an

6 It's from Pol.and　　　　　It's Pol.ish

7 So you're from Hun.gar.y　　So you're Hun.gar.i.an

🎧 **1.6 Check your answers. Then listen again, and practise the sentences.**

Conversations

A **Match each item on the left with a suitable response on the right.**

1 Hello.
2 Nice to meet you, Tim.
3 This is Andrea. She's in Marketing.
4 How's business?
5 Are you in Marketing, too?
6 See you later.
7 How about some tea?
8 Business is not very good.
9 Are you from Argentina?
10 Is your company Swiss?

a) Pleased to meet you, Andrea. I'm Liz.
b) No, it isn't. It's French.
c) Hi!
d) Oh, thanks. I'd love some.
e) Yes, I am. I live in Buenos Aires.
f) And you.
g) No, I'm not. I'm in Human Resources.
h) Fine, thanks.
i) Right. Bye now!
j) Oh, I'm sorry to hear that.

B **Complete the conversation with items from the box.**

~~name's~~ Sales how's Pleased I'm Are Manager meet

A: Hello. My ...*name's*... Francis – Francis Wells. .... the new accountant.

B: Hi! I'm Tom Murphy. Nice to .... you, Francis.

A: .... to meet you, Tom. .... you in Accounts, too?

B: No, I'm not. I'm in .... I'm Assistant Sales ....

A: Mm, that's interesting. And .... business?

B: Not too bad, not too bad.

🎧 1.7 **Listen and check your answers. Then listen again and practise Speaker B's part.**

Listening practice

C 🎧 1.8 **Listen and tick the best answer a), b) or c) for each question.**

1 a) Yes, I am.
 b) No, he's Russian.
 c) Yes, he is. ✔

2 a) Yes, I work in Marketing.
 b) Yes, it's in Finland.
 c) This is my mobile phone.

3 a) No, I'm not. I'm an engineer.
 b) Yes. I live and work in Grenoble.
 c) Yes, she is.

4 a) Pleased to meet you, too.
 b) Well, I'm interested in travel.
 c) Yes, and I've got two children.

5 a) Yes. Her name's Luisa.
 b) No, my brother's an engineer.
 c) Not too bad, thanks.

6 a) No, they're Japanese.
 b) Yes. They're from Osaka, in fact.
 c) They like soccer.

7 a) Yes. We drink a lot of coffee.
 b) Me too.
 c) Thanks very much. I'd love one.

8 a) No, it isn't. It's Swiss, actually.
 b) I'm from Stuttgart. How about you?
 c) No. They're engineers.

UNIT 2 — Work and leisure

A 🎧 **2.1 Listen to how the verbs are pronounced.**

one syllable	likes	works
two syllables	o.pens	watch.es
three syllables	tel.e.phones	fin.ish.es

B 🎧 **2.2 Listen to the recording. How many syllables do you hear?**

1 travels ....*2*......　　5 delivers ....

2 discusses ....　　6 visits ....

3 starts ....　　7 changes ....

4 closes ....　　8 completes ....

🎧 **2.2 Listen again and practise saying the words.**

C Put the words from the box in the correct column, according to the pronunciation of the letter(s) in bold.

~~Fr**i**day~~	~~w**i**nter~~	n**igh**t	off**i**ce	cl**i**ent	Sw**i**ss
des**ig**n	d**i**nner	c**y**cling	arr**i**ve		

/ɪ/ as in *quick fix*	/aɪ/ as in *my price*
winter	Friday

🎧 **2.3 Listen and check your answers. Then listen again and practise the words.**

Connected speech

D 🎧 **2.4 Listen to the way certain words can be linked.**

a large‿office　in‿a large‿office　He works‿in‿a large‿office

E 🎧 **2.5 Listen to these sentences and show the links that you hear.**

1 He works until 8 o'clock.

2 He's interested in advertising.

3 She gets up at 6 and does exercises.

4 She does a lot of overtime.

5 He has a lot of meetings in the afternoon.

🎧 **2.5 Check your answers. Then listen again and practise the sentences.**

What's the rule?

When a word finishes with a **consonant** and the word immediately after begins with a **vowel** sound, we usually link those two words.

Questions and answers

A Complete the interview with questions from the box.

> **a)** How often do you have breaks?
> **b)** What hours do you work?
> **c)** ... So, what's your job?
> **d)** When and where do you have lunch?
> **e)** What do you not like about your job?
> **f)** And what exactly do you do?

Interviewer: ...*C*....[1]

Ana Ross: I'm Assistant Project Manager.

Interviewer: ....[2]

Ana Ross: I spend a lot of time with our clients. I make a lot of phone calls, and I write lots of e-mails.

Interviewer: ....[3]

Ana Ross: Well, it's a 9 to 5 job, but I usually arrive at 8:30, and I often stay until 6, sometimes later.

Interviewer: ....[4]

Ana Ross: When I'm not too busy, I sometimes have a short coffee break at 10:30 and at 3:30. And then there's lunch, of course.

Interviewer: ....[5]

Ana Ross: Lunch is at 12:45. I never miss it! Our cafeteria is very good.

Interviewer: ....[6]

Ana Ross: The hours are too long, but it's all right. I love my job, and my colleagues are fantastic.

Listening practice

B 🎧 2.6 **Look at the questions below. Listen and choose the best answer a), b) or c) for each question.**

1   How often do you write reports? | *c* |
2   Do you travel a lot for work?
3   What time do you usually finish?
4   What do you like best about your job?
5   How's business?
6   Are you from Estonia?
7   What do you do in your free time?
8   How many hours a week do you work?
9   How often do you have meetings?
10 What do you want from work?

UNIT 3 Problems

Individual sounds

A 🎧 **3.1 Listen to how the letter _a_ is pronounced in the following words.**

late	want	carry	can't

B 🎧 **3.2 Listen and complete the words.**

/eɪ/ as in _play safe_	/ɒ/ as in _top job_	/æ/ as in _bad bank_	/ɑː/ as in _smart card_
1 d a ng e r o us	4 ___ lity	7 _r_vel	10 h__d
2 s__ce	5 w__ch	8 __g	11 ___t
3 del___d	6 __ft	9 n___ow	12 f_s_

🎧 **3.2 Listen again and practise the words.**

C 🎧 **3.3 Listen to these words. Then complete the sentence.**

manager   package   damaged

In these words, the second letter _a_ is pronounced / ... / as in .... (See page 52.)

Connected speech

D 🎧 **3.4 Listen to how _do you_ is pronounced in these questions.**

Do you live in a city?   How often do you travel abroad?
Do you go to meetings?   What do you do?

> **Tip**
>
> A lot of people pronounce _do you_ (= two words) as /djə/. That's why it often sounds like one word.

E 🎧 **3.5 Listen and complete the questions.**

1 Do you .... to work?
2 What time .... you start work?
3 When do .... finish work?
4 Who do you .... to?
5 .... do you do so much overtime?

🎧 **3.5 Listen again and practise asking the questions.**

Stress and intonation

F 🎧 **3.6 Listen to these questions. Notice the stress on the two important words.**

Do you <u>work</u> in an <u>office</u>?
Do you <u>travel</u> a <u>lot</u>?

G **Mark the two main stresses in the following questions.**

1 Do you work in August?
2 Do you socialise with colleagues?
3 Do you like your job?

🎧 **3.7 Listen and check your answers. Then listen again and practise asking the questions.**

Sound work

What's the problem?

A 3.8 **Listen and complete the sentences about problems.**

1 We'll have to walk, I'm afraid. The ...*lift*...... is out of order.

2 I can't do the photocopying. We've run out of A4 .... Where can I get some?

3 The coffee .... is broken. Let's get a new one.

4 I think there's something wrong with their .... The line is engaged all the time.

5 The .... isn't working properly. The paper jams every time I use it.

6 There's a .... stain on this envelope. Can I have another one, please?

B Look at exercise A and underline the phrases used to talk about problems.

C Put these sentences in the correct order to make a telephone conversation.

a) Goodbye. ☐

b) Good morning. Belco Electronics. How can I help you? ☐ *1*

c) It's Flat 3, 18 Duke Road. ☐

d) Oh, I'm very sorry to hear that. It's the *Max 3000* you bought yesterday, is it? ☐

e) Right. I've got that. I'll put an instructions manual in the post for you straight away. And once again, sorry about our mistake. ☐

f) Good morning. Steve Jenkins here. Well, it's about the *Max 3000* computer software. I'm afraid there are no instructions in the box. ☐

g) Thank you very much. Goodbye. ☐

h) Well, Mr Jenkins, just give me your address, and I'll send you the instructions. ☐

i) Yes, that's right. ☐

3.9 **Listen and check your answers. Then listen again and practise Steve's responses.**

Listening practice

D 3.10 **Listen and tick the best answer a), b) or c) for each question.**

1 a) Speaking. How can I help you? ✓

   b) No, thanks. Not today.

   c) Yes, of course. What's the model number?

2 a) Well, my air conditioner is out of order too.

   b) I know. It's a very good machine.

   c) I'm sorry to hear that. What seems to be the problem?

3 a) Is the printer broken?

   b) Could you give us some details, please?

   c) All your invoices are incorrect.

4 a) Yes. I finish work at 6:30.

   b) The instructions are missing and some parts are broken.

   c) I'm sorry. All the trains are delayed. It's terrible!

5 a) Well, I think they're unhappy here. That's the problem.

   b) I don't think there's enough space.

   c) Because they don't go to meetings.

6 a) I'm afraid she's in a meeting just now. Would you like to leave a message?

   b) I'm sorry to hear that.

   c) Hello. Bob Lyons here. I'd like to speak to the manager, please.

UNIT 4   Travel

Individual sounds

A 🎧 **4.1 Listen to how the letter _o_ is pronounced in the following words.**

office   home   m**o**ney   airp**o**rt   c**o**llect

B **Put the words in exercise A in the correct column, according to the pronunciation of the letters in bold.**

/ə/ as in _about Canada_	/əʊ/ as in _go slow_	/ɒ/ as in _top job_	/ɔː/ as in _short course_	/ʌ/ as in _much luck_
collect	....	....	....	....
....	....	....	....	....

C **Put each word in the correct column in exercise B.**

pass**po**rt   c**o**nfirm   h**o**tel   c**o**me   sh**o**p

🎧 **4.2 Now check your answers. Then listen again and practise the words.**

Connected speech

D 🎧 **4.3 Listen to the recording. Are the sentences positive (+) or negative (-)?**

1 ...+...   5 ......

2 ...−...   6 ......

3 ......   7 ......

4 ......   8 ......

Now check your answers.

Have you noticed?

           O[1]

You   can   come.

     /kən/

        O   O

They   can't   go.

     /kɑːnt/

[1] A big circle above a word shows that the word is stressed.

🎧 **4.3 Listen again and practise the sentences.**

Stress and intonation

E 🎧 **4.4 Listen and complete these polite requests.**

1 Can I ..._use_...... the phone, please?

2 Can I have a .... , please?

3 Can I have the ...., please?

4 Can I have a glass of ...., please?

5 Can I take one of these ...., please?

6 Can I .... an alarm call at 6:15, please?

🎧 **4.4 Listen again and practise the polite intonation used by the speakers.**

Sound work

Using stress to correct information

A 🎧 4.5 **Listen to the recording and complete these telephone conversations.**

1 A: So the first name is spelt F-R-A-N-C-I-S.

  B: No. It's ....

2 A: And the phone number is 3228 5959.

  B: Sorry, no. It's ....

3 A: Ms Salgado's flight number is IP3208.

  B: Can you check that again, please? The number I have here is
  ....

🎧 4.5 **Listen again and notice how Speaker B uses stress to correct Speaker A.**

No. It's F-R-A-N-C-E̱-S.

Sorry, no. It's 3228 5̱8̱59.

The number I have here is I̱Ḇ3208.

B **Look at these telephone conversations. Underline the part that Speaker B needs to stress to correct Speaker A.**

1 A: So you need two single rooms for three nights, from the twenty-third of this month?

  B: No. We need them from the twenty-first.

2 A: Right. One double room with shower for two nights.

  B: Sorry. I'd like one with bath, if possible.

3 A: ... and an aisle seat for Ms Sandra Davis. D-A-V-I-S ...

  B: Sorry, no. D-A-V-I-E-S.

4 A: The train leaves from platform eighteen, is that right?

  B: No sir. You want platform sixteen for Newcastle.

5 A: Is the fitness centre on the ground floor?

  B: No, madam. It's on the fourth floor.

6 A: Let me just write this down ... Two hundred and fifty euros, and ...

  B: Sorry, no. That's two hundred and thirty euros.

🎧 4.6 **Listen to the recording. Then listen again, check your answers and practise Speaker B's replies.**

Listening practice

C 🎧 4.7 **Look at questions 1–10 below. Listen and choose the best response a), b) or c) for each question.**

1 What time does his train arrive? | *b* |

2 Is it a room with a good view of the sea?

3 Can I use the phone, please?

4 How far is it from the airport to the hotel?

5 Are there any flights to Vancouver after eight?

6 Have you got any rooms?

7 Can I have a receipt, please?

8 What's the flight number?

9 Can I have an alarm call at 5 a.m., please?

10 Which terminal do Qatar Airways flights leave from?

Survival business English

UNIT 5 Food and entertaining

Individual sounds

A 🎧 **5.1 Listen to the difference between /ɪ/ and /iː/ .**

/ɪ/	/iː/
Tim	team
sit	seat

B Put the words from the box into the correct column, according to the pronunciation of the letter(s) in bold.

~~sw**ee**t~~ b**i**ll man**a**ger m**ea**l rec**ei**pt ch**i**cken bus**i**ness Sw**e**den

/ɪ/ as in quick f**i**x	/iː/ as in cl**ea**n sh**ee**t
....	*sweet*
....	....
....	....
....	....

🎧 **5.2 Check your answers. Then listen and practise saying the words.**

Connected speech

C 🎧 **5.3 Listen and complete the sentences.**
1 It's ... *for* .... you.
2 How about .... dessert?
3 Why don't we invite them .... dinner?
4 Would you like .... more juice?
5 How much time do you have .... lunch?
6 There aren't a lot .... restaurants in this area.
7 What do you recommend .... the main course?
8 They have a lot .... fish dishes on the menu.

> **Tip**
>
> We normally use the weak forms /fə/, /səm/, /əv/ when *for*, *some* or *of* are within the sentence.

🎧 **5.3 Listen again and practise saying the sentences.**

Stress and intonation

D Put the words from the box into four groups according to their stress pattern.

~~spaghetti~~ ~~service~~ ~~company~~ ~~dessert~~ business delicious menu receipt restaurant

O o	o O	O o o	o O o
service	*dessert*	*company*	*spaghetti*
....	....	....	....
....	....	....	....

🎧 **5.4 Listen and check your answers. Then listen again and practise saying the words.**

Sound work

Eating out

A **Dieter is taking Bob, a colleague from Ireland, out to dinner in Frankfurt. Complete Dieter's questions with words and phrases from the box.**

~~Do you~~	Are	how about	How's	Shall
	Shall we	would you	you like	

1 ...*Do you*....... like Italian food?
2 .... I ask for a menu in English?
3 .... you ready to order?
4 What .... like for the main course?
5 .... your food?
6 Now, Bob, ... a dessert?
7 Would .... to have coffee or tea?
8 Right. .... get the bill?

🎧 **5.5 Listen and check your answers.**

B **Match each of Bob's answers to one of Dieter's questions in exercise A.**

a) I think I need a few more minutes. ..*3*....
b) Mm, yeah. I'd love an espresso, actually. ....
c) Mm. Some lasagna would be nice. ....
d) No, thanks. I don't really like sweet things. ....
e) No, that's all right, thanks. I need to practise my German a bit. ....
f) Oh yes, I love it. ....
g) Yes, let's. It's getting late. ....
h) Very nice, thank you. We must come here again next time I'm in Frankfurt. ....

🎧 **5.6 Listen and check your answers. Then listen and practise Dieter's part.**

Listening practice

C 🎧 **5.7 A businessman is entertaining some colleagues at home. Listen and tick the most appropriate answer a), b) or c) for each question that you hear.**

1 a) It's delicious.
  b) Yes, thanks, that's fine. ✔
  c) I say enough is enough.

2 a) No. Give me more meat.
  b) Yes, please.
  c) Ice with fish? No, thanks.

3 a) Erm ... Some mineral water would be nice.
  b) No, thanks. I'm fine.
  c) I want some fruit juice.

4 a) I like fish, but I don't like eggs.
  b) Just a little, please. It's delicious.
  c) OK.

5 a) Yes, there's enough for everybody.
  b) No, but we have orange juice.
  c) Yes, of course. Here you are.

6 a) No, thanks. It was lovely, but I'm full.
  b) Yes, of course.
  c) Oh no, please.

Survival business English

UNIT 6 — Sales

Individual sounds

A Match the past forms which contain the same sound.

1 grew
2 bought
3 gave
4 got
5 said
6 sold
7 took

a) cost
b) met
c) knew
d) caught
e) paid
f) put
g) wrote

🎧 **6.1 Listen and check your answers. Then listen again and practise saying the words.**

B 🎧 **6.2 Listen and complete the sentences with the form of the verb *to be* that you hear.**

1 Delivery *is* .... free.
2 There .... no extra cost.
3 How much .... they?
4 It .... a great deal.
5 They........ at the office.
6 We .... away on business.
7 These models .... easy to use.
8 The design........ interesting.
9 We........ looking for experienced sales reps.
10 They .... on time.

Have you noticed?

are/'re		/ ə (r) /
was	is often pronounced	/ w ə z /
were		/ w ə (r) /

Stress and intonation

C Put the verbs from the box in the correct column according to their stress pattern.

advised   expanded   exported   finished   improved   ~~launched~~
needed   offered   promoted   received   stopped   worked

1 O talked	2 O o started	3 o O increased	4 o O o invited
launched			

🎧 **6.3 Listen and check your answers. Then listen again and practice saying the words.**

Sales talk

A 6.4 **Listen to these extracts from product presentations and complete the sentences.**

1 The *Tex23* is our most *popular* laptop computer bag. It's ....
for the business traveller, and it's available in black or dark brown leather.

2 *LockIt* is an excellent protection against car crime. It's ....
of steel and is very strong.

3 With our new *Medico* testing kit, busy executives get useful and ....
information about their health. It's .... to use because it's fully
automatic. And it's so small you can carry it in your briefcase.

4 The *Dual EM* mobile phone is in the low price .... , but it has a
lot of special .... For example, you can read and write e-mail
messages anywhere in the world.

5 Made for busy office people, the *Exex* desk chair is .... and
very well designed. *Exex* is the solution to your back problems.

6 With the *Storage Wizard* you can find any of your CDs or CD-ROMs quickly
and easily. It's a very .... storage system that saves a lot of
.... and a lot of time.

Listening practice

B 6.5 **A salesperson is answering some customers' questions. Listen and tick the most appropriate answer a), b) or c) for each question that you hear.**

1 a) No, but you can pay a deposit.
  b) Yes. Six percent on large orders.
  c) Yes. It's one year on all models. ✔

2 a) Yes. So we could deliver any time this week.
  b) They are very good indeed – the best on the market.
  c) Well, I'll contact you again tomorrow.

3 a) Yes, if you can give us a 10% discount.
  b) Yes, of course. But then there's a 10% deposit to pay.
  c) I'm afraid those models are no longer in stock.

4 a) It's available in small, medium, or large.
  b) We can deliver it within three days.
  c) We stock it in white, green and blue.

5 a) Yes, they always deliver on time.
  b) Yes. It's waterproof.
  c) €400, delivery included.

6 a) Yes, of course.
  b) No, we don't need to compare prices.
  c) Well, they're in the medium price range.

7 a) It's for anyone who wants a healthy lifestyle.
  b) Exactly. It's a very competitive market.
  c) It's for a limited period only.

8 a) The delivery date was Thursday.
  b) The trade price was €240.
  c) We offer free delivery within ten days.

Survival business English

UNIT 7   People

Individual sounds

A 🎧 **7.1 Listen and add the missing letters to the words.**

1 s_p_end   _ _ _ead   _ _ _ing
2 _ _aff   _ _ _ess   _ _ _ong
3 _ _ill   _ _ _een   _ _ _i_ _
4 _ _a_ _ical   _ _o_ _em   _ _a_ _ise
5 he_ _ _ul   pu_ _ _ual
6 i_ _ _ease   e_ _a_ _

Tip

Many English words have groups of two or three consonants at the beginning, in the middle or at the end of words. Pronounce those consonants clearly together, without adding any other sound before or between them.

🎧 **7.1 Listen and check your answers. Then listen again and practise saying the words. Pay attention in particular to the groups of consonants.**

Connected speech

B 🎧 **7.2 Listen to the way certain words can be linked.**

an‿office   in‿an‿office   He works‿in‿an‿office.

C 🎧 **7.3 Listen to these sentences and show the links that you hear.**

1 I met Edit in April.
2 I didn't send it out on time.
3 She got on well with others.
4 He had a lot of interesting ideas.
5 It was a bad idea to sell it.

🎧 **7.3 Check your answers. Then listen again and practise the sentences.**

D 🎧 **7.4 Listen and practise giving short answers to the questions.**

1 Yes, he ...._was_........ .
2 No, she ..._didn't_......... .
3 Yes, they ....
4 No, we ....
5 No, ...
6 Yes, ...

Stress and intonation

E 🎧 **7.5 Listen to these questions. Notice the stresses, and notice how the voice goes down at the end.**

    O   O   O ↘
1 How did you get to the office?

    O   O   O ↘
2 Where did she start her journey?

    O   O   O ↘
3 When did they found the company?

    O O ↘
4 How old were they?

    O O ↘
5 How far was it?

Tip

In *wh-* questions, the voice often goes down at the end.

🎧 **7.5 Listen again and practise saying the questions.**

Sound work

Management issues

A Complete the sentences with the correct word from the box.

| ~~costs~~ | down | leave | manage | suggestion | too |

1 I think we should try and keep _costs_ down.
2 There's .... much work for the staff.
3 Sales are .... again this month, I'm afraid.
4 The problem is, she doesn't know how to .... people.
5 Can I make a .... ? I think we should hire some more staff.
6 I think he should .... the company. He's making everyone unhappy.

B Match the following responses to the sentences in exercise A.
a) Everybody says so. And she doesn't support her staff at all. ☐ 4
b) I agree. We are spending far too much. ☐
c) I know they work very hard, but we haven't got the money to employ more people, I'm afraid. ☐
d) That's a good idea. Two or three part-time workers would make life easier for us. ☐
e) Yeah. Every day there are complaints about his behaviour. ☐
f) Yes. Business is bad. ☐

C 7.6 Listen to eight extracts from negotiations and decide what each speaker is doing.
Write one letter, a)– d), next to the number of the speaker. Use each letter twice.

Speaker 1: ..... _b_ ....   a) Describing a problem
Speaker 2: ....   b) Responding
Speaker 3: ....   c) Making a suggestion
Speaker 4: ....   d) Explaining the reasons
Speaker 5: ....
Speaker 6: ....
Speaker 7: ....
Speaker 8: ....

Listening practice

D 7.7 Look at items 1–6 below. Listen and choose the best response a), b) or c) for each item.
1 Why was Daniel so difficult to work with? ☐ d
2 I need support to do my job. ☐
3 Does Peter give his colleagues any problems? ☐
4 Your staff are off sick all the time. What's the problem? ☐
5 There's a lot of work. I really need an assistant. ☐
6 We simply don't have enough staff. ☐

Survival business English

UNIT 8   Markets

Individual sounds

A 🎧 8.1 Listen to the *schwa* sound (ə) in these words (see page 52).

o O	o O o	O o o
ma.ture /ə/	a.ttract.ive /ə/	qual.it.y /ə/
suc.cess /ə/	con.sum.er /ə/ /ə/	hol.i.day /ə/

Tip

Notice that non-stressed syllables often have /ə/.

🎧 8.1 Listen to the words again and practise saying them.

Connected speech

B 🎧 8.2 Listen to the *schwa* sound in these comparative forms.

1 bett**er**   bett**er** th**a**n   It's bett**er** th**a**n last month.
2 cheap**er**   cheap**er** th**a**n   Life is cheap**er** here th**a**n in Paris.
3 heavi**er**   heavi**er** th**a**n   This model is heavi**er** th**a**n the RT100.

Tip

Notice that the ending *-er* is pronounced /ə/ and *than* is pronounced /ðən/.

🎧 8.2 Listen to the examples again and practise saying them.

C 🎧 8.3 Listen and write the last three words of each sentence.

1 Our market share is increasing faster here ......*than*.. ......*in*..... ....*Korea*... .
2 The Hilton is bigger ....
3 Our main competitor offers a cheaper service ....
....
4 The rate of unemployment is worse ....
5 She's more popular ....

🎧 8.3 Listen again and practise the sentences.

Stress and intonation

D Look at the example and explanation. Then underline the word which has a different stress pattern in each line below.

Example:

declining   expensive   <u>luxury</u>

Explanation: we say deCLIning and exPENsive (stress on the second syllable) but LUXury (stress on the first syllable).

1 marketing   attractive   company
2 quality   department   producer
3 profitable   competitive   comfortable
4 thousand   million   percent
5 market   mature   success

🎧 8.4 Listen and check your answers. Then listen again and practise saying the words.

Sound work

Meetings

A Put the words in the right order to make sentences often used in meetings.

1 think / you're / I / right   *I think you're right.*

2 agree / I'm / I / afraid / don't

3 about / you / this / How / feel / do / ?

4 the / really / I / idea / like

5 about / May / re-launching / in / What / it / ?

🎧 **8.5 Listen and check your answers. Then listen again and practise the sentences.**

B Match the following language functions to the sentences in exercise A.

a) Asking for an opinion $\boxed{3}$

b) Agreeing $\boxed{}$ $\boxed{}$

c) Disagreeing $\boxed{}$

d) Making a suggestion $\boxed{}$

C Put these opening sentences from a meeting in the right order.

a) **Liz:** Fine. That makes our work easier. And what income group? $\boxed{}$

b) **Sue:** Hmm. I'm not sure about that. Teenagers don't find this kind of design attractive. $\boxed{}$

c) **Sue:** I suggest the middle and lower income groups. We have a quality product, and we want it to be a bit cheaper than our competitors'. $\boxed{}$

d) **Liz:** So let's start then. My first question is, which market segment should we choose? $\boxed{1}$

e) **Tom:** Well, I think we should target tennis players, in all age groups. $\boxed{}$

f) **Tom:** You're probably right. Let's target men and women in the age group 25-plus, then. $\boxed{}$

Listening practice

D 🎧 **8.6 Listen and tick the most appropriate answer a), b) or c).**

1 a) Yes. You are right.

  b) Well, I think sales are better than for other products.

  c) In airport and railway station shops. ✔

2 a) I think we should target single men and women in the upper income group.

  b) Central Europe is the main target.

  c) Well, consumer behaviour is different here.

3 a) Not on TV or radio this time!

  b) We should advertise more.

  c) Let's start the campaign in August.

4 a) Our market share is very small.

  b) Yes, they are the market leader in that area.

  c) Well, the price isn't quite right.

5 a) Let's re-launch it under a different brand name.

  b) At the end of the summer holiday.

  c) I'm afraid I don't agree.

6 a) Yes. We should target middle-aged women.

  b) Yes. Let's do more market research next year.

  c) Sales always go down in winter.

UNIT 9   Companies

A   **Underline the silent letter(s) in the following words.**

a<u>i</u>sle	debt	island	salmon
answer	fasten	know	sandwich
autumn	foreign	lamb	talk
climb	half	receipt	Wednesday

9.1 Listen and check your answers. Then listen again and practise saying the words.

Connected speech

B   **9.2 Listen to the pronunciation of the word *are* in these sentences.**

1   We <u>are</u> looking for a bigger warehouse.
     /ə/
2   Five companies <u>are</u> competing for this contract.
     /ə/
3   Our profit figures <u>are</u>‿improving.
     /ər/
4   Many German companies <u>are</u>‿investing in Turkey.
     /ər/

Tips

1   Notice that *are* is often pronounced /ə/ or /ər/.
2   you are = you're   we are = we're   they are = they're
•   The meaning is the same.
•   The contracted forms are not used in formal business correspondence.

9.2 Listen to the examples again and practise saying them.

C   **9.3 Listen and complete the sentences.**

1   ....*You 're opening*.. a subsidiary in Toulouse, is that right?
2   ....' .... setting up joint ventures with Chinese companies.
3   What .... research into?
4   Our competitors .... abroad.
5   What .... to achieve?
6   .... looking for new offices?

9.3 Listen again and practise the sentences.

D   **9.4 Listen to the pronunciation of the underlined words.**

1   We <u>aren't</u> looking for new markets.   3   Our turnover <u>isn't</u> increasing.
2   They <u>aren't</u> competing for that contract.   4   She <u>isn't</u> working tomorrow.

Tips

I am not = I'm not   is not = isn't   are not = aren't
•   The meaning is the same.
•   The contracted forms are not used in formal business correspondence.

9.4 Listen to the examples again and practise saying them.

E 🎧 9.5 **Listen and complete the sentences with the contracted forms.**

1 ..*They*.... ...*aren't*.... investing in Indonesia.
2 .... planning to start a new business.
3 .... attracting a lot of new customers.
4 .... growing very fast.
5 .... launching it until September.

Talks and presentations

A **Match the sentence halves.**

1 As you know, I'm here today to tell you
2 Firstly, I'd like to look at our
3 Good afternoon. I'd like to welcome you all
4 Hi, everyone. Good to see
5 My talk today is
6 What I'd like to do today is to

a) present our new products.
b) in three main parts.
c) performance over the last three months.
d) about our new joint venture in Turkey.
e) you all. My name's Rita Horvath.
f) here this afternoon.

B **Put the sentences from exercise A under the correct heading.**

Greeting the audience	Introducing the topic	Giving a plan of the talk
.*3 and*....	....*and*....	....*and*....

Listening practice

C 🎧 9.6 **After each conversation, read the question and tick the correct answer.**

1 What kind of building does the man's company want?
   a) A larger one.
   b) A cheaper one.
   c) A smaller one.

2 What is the man's opinion of the February sales figures?
   a) They were better last month.
   b) They are better than in January.
   c) They aren't much better this month.

3 Which one of these statements is true?
   a) Tom and Chris are in Azerbaijan to start a joint venture.
   b) The woman doesn't know what she's talking about.
   c) Chris wants to negotiate a contract.

4 Which part of the woman's presentation will be about the features of the new product?
   a) The first.
   b) The second.
   c) The third.

5 What do the man and the woman agree about?
   a) Sales figures are going down.
   b) They need to work harder.
   c) The marketing strategy is not good.

UNIT 10   The Web

Individual sounds

A 🎧 10.1 **Listen to the difference between /v/ and /w/.**

/ v /	/ w /
video	win
value	way

B 🎧 10.2 **Complete the sentences with the words you hear.**

1 Their *website* is *very* exciting.

2 In my ...., it's a .... of money.

3 .... site do you .... most often?

4 The .... Wide Web is of great .... to advertisers.

5 If you .... to .... that site, you need a valid password.

6 I received a .... warning.

🎧 10.2 **Listen to the sentences again and practise saying them.**

Connected speech

C 🎧 10.3 **Listen and tick the sentences that you hear.**

1 We take the early flight.   We'll take the early flight. ✔

2 They work hard.   They'll work hard.

3 I do it for them.   I'll do it for them.

4 You have to download it.   You'll have to download it.

5 They buy the same software.   They'll buy the same software.

6 We try all the search engines.   We'll try all the search engines.

D 🎧 10.4 **Listen to the pronunciation of the contracted forms.**

1 **I'll** show you.   4 **She'll** buy them.

2 **You'll** need it.   5 **We'll** watch it.

3 **He'll** want one.   6 **They'll** do it.

🎧 10.4 **Listen to the examples again and practise saying them.**

Stress and intonation

E 🎧 10.5 **Listen to these conversations. Notice how Speaker B uses stress to correct Speaker A.**

1 **A:** So the flight's boarding at Gate 30.

   B: No, it's Gate 13 we want.

2 **A:** Right. So I can come any Tuesday.

   B: Sorry, no. I said any Thursday.

F **Look at these conversations. Underline the part that Speaker B will stress to correct Speaker A in each case.**

1 **A:** ... and you said check-in is at nine o'clock.

   B: No, it's eight o'clock, I'm afraid.

2 **A:** ... so that's Janet G-R-A-Y.

   B: Sorry, no. G-R-E-Y. Mrs Janet Grey.

3 **A:** Excuse me. Is the presentation on the first floor?

   B: No, it's on the third floor. You'd better take the lift.

4 **A:** ... and your e-mail address is Vermeulen@pe.org.

   B: That's not quite right. It's B-E, as in Belgium.

Sound work

5 A: Let me just read the postcode back to you: CM20 3GE.

   B: No. It's CM20 3JE.

6 A: So the fax number of their Sofia office is 359 2 968 61 58.

   B: ... 61 98.

🎧 **10.6 Listen and check your answers. Then listen again, and practise Speaker B's replies.**

Making arrangements

Ⓐ 🎧 **10.7 Listen to ten extracts from conversations and decide what each speaker is doing.**
Write one letter, a)–e), next to the number of the speaker. Use each letter twice.

Speaker 1: ....*b*..............   **a)** Asking

Speaker 2: ....   **b)** Agreeing

Speaker 3: ....   **c)** Declining

Speaker 4: ....   **d)** Suggesting a different time

Speaker 5: ....   **e)** Apologising

Speaker 6: ....

Speaker 7: ....

Speaker 8: ....

Speaker 9: ....

Speaker 10: ....

Listening practice

Ⓑ 🎧 **10.8 After each conversation, read the question and tick the correct answer, a), b) or c).**

1 When are they going to discuss the contract?

  a) Monday.

  b) Tuesday.

  c) Wednesday. ✓

2 Why does the man sound disappointed? Because:

  a) they just talked.

  b) people were worried.

  c) the woman wasn't there.

3 How is the man going to the airport?

  a) By metro.

  b) By car.

  c) By taxi.

4 What does the man want Sandra to do?

  a) Come to a meeting.

  b) Come back before 11:30.

  c) Phone him later.

5 Why is the man late? Because:

  a) all flights were half an hour late.

  b) he waited a long time at baggage reclaim.

  c) the weather was bad.

6 Where and when are they going to meet?

  a) In the cafeteria at 9:00.

  b) At the registration desk at 10:00.

  c) In the cafeteria after the conference.

UNIT 11 **Cultures**

Individual sounds

A 🎧 **11.1 Listen and add the missing letters to the words.**

1 firs t   reque_ _ _   ho_ _ _

2 _ _aff   _ _ore   _ _ _ategy

3 _ _eak   _ _ace   _ _e_ _ _ _

4 _ _ar_ _   _ _o_ _ _ _   _ _ _i_ _

5 _ _or_ _   _ _iri_ _   _ _eciali_ _ _

Tip

Many English words have groups of two or three consonant sounds at the beginning, in the middle or at the end of words. Pronounce those consonant sounds clearly together, without adding any other sound before or between them.

🎧 **11.1 Listen again and practise saying the words. Pay attention in particular to the groups of consonant sounds.**

Connected speech

B 🎧 **11.2 Listen and complete the sentences with *should* or *shouldn't*.**

1 In Finland, you ... *should* ... never arrive late for an appointment.

2 In many countries, you .... write on business cards.

3 You .... offer your hand to shake immediately.

4 In Germany, you .... use the person's title before the surname.

5 In most countries, you .... point your finger at the person you're talking to.

6 So, before you go to a new country, you .... do your homework!

🎧 **11.2 Listen again and practise saying the sentences.**

C **Put the words from the box in the correct column according to their stress pattern.**

important popular ~~silence~~ arrive offer document arrangement adapt

1 O o	2 o O	3 O o o	4 o O o
custom /ə/ *silence*	abroad /ə/	cultural /ə/ə/	appointment /ə/ /ə/ ....

🎧 **11.3 Listen and check your answers.**

D **Listen to the words in exercise C again and write the /ə/ sounds that you hear. Then check your answers.**

Do you remember?

All the /ə/ sounds are in the unstressed syllables (see 8.1 for more examples).

🎧 **11.3 Listen again and practise saying the words.**

Stress and intonation

E 🎧 **11.4 Tick the offers and requests where the speaker sounds polite.**

1 Could I use your phone? ✔

2 Could I use your computer? ✘

3 Would you like a drink?

4 Would you like a sandwich?

5 Could you tell me the way?

6 Could you check these figures?

Check your answers.

F 🎧 **11.5 Listen to these polite offers and requests. Practise saying them.**

1 Would you like some coffee?

2 Could you spell that for me?

3 Could I use the meeting room?

4 Would you like a copy of the brochure?

5 Could you make the travel arrangements for me?

6 Could I borrow your dictionary?

Dialogues

A **Two managers are talking about a problem. Complete the dialogues with items from the box.**

> a) Explain to them *why* we changed the schedule.
>
> b) And try to find out exactly what each one of them is unhappy about.
>
> c) I'll try that.
>
> d) They're complaining about our new work schedule.
>
> e) But, unfortunately, they still don't agree with a lot of the changes.
>
> f) ~~What kind of problems?~~

A: So you're saying there are problems in Sales. ..*f*...

B: Well, it's the representatives. . . . . . .

A: Do you know what the best thing to do is? . . . . . .

B: I think they understand the reasons. . . . . . .

A: Well, maybe you should talk to them one by one. . . . . . .

B: OK then. . . . . . .

🎧 **11.6 Listen to the dialogue and check your answers.**

Listening practice

B 🎧 **11.7 Listen and tick the most appropriate response a), b) or c).**

1 a) I really don't know. You should ask Tina – she's worked in Vietnam before. ✔

  b) That's right. I'll call everyone Friday morning.

  c) Of course! You should always telephone first.

2 a) Yes. The last meeting was late in the afternoon, too.

  b) All right. Just let me know when the next one is.

  c) Well, he doesn't enjoy the work here, I'm afraid.

3 a) That's right, yeah. Never write on a business card.

  b) Yes. Always offer and receive things with your right hand.

  c) Yes, please. And I'll give you mine.

4 a) Well, normally we have a holiday in the summer.

  b) Much the same as here. Most people have a 9 to 5 job.

  c) No, not many people work from home.

5 a) Yes. People speak Portuguese in Brazil, you know.

  b) Good idea. We need to communicate more.

  c) Try the Internet. The *Lonely Planet* website, for example.

6 a) Most young people now drink Italian-style coffee.

  b) No, thanks. Just some water.

  c) Well, in the morning I usually have orange juice and cereal.

Survival business English

UNIT 12   Jobs

Individual sounds

A 🎧 **12.1 Listen to the difference between /ɒ/ and /ɔː/.**

/ɒ/	/ɔː/
not	nought
spot	sport
top job	short course

B **Underline all the letters that are pronounced /ɔː/ in these sentences.**

1 How often do you write reports?

2 What sorts of bosses have you had?

3 Our office staff don't wear uniforms.

4 Robert has taught abroad for four years.

🎧 **12.2 Listen and check your answers. Then listen again and practise saying the sentences.**

Connected speech

C 🎧 **12.3 Listen and complete the sentences. Use contractions ('s / 've / hasn't / haven't).**

1 _She's_ gained a lot of experience.

2 .... finished everything.

3 .... sent his CV.

4 .... invited her for an interview.

5 .... selected anyone.

6 .... interviewed everyone.

🎧 **12.3 Listen again, and practise saying the sentences.**

D 🎧 **12.4 Listen to the way has(n't) and have(n't) are pronounced in questions and short answers.**

/həvjə/

A: Have you ever worked in a bank?

B: Yes, I have.

/hæv/

/həzʃi/

A: Has she done anything that shows leadership?

B: Yes, I think she has.

/hæz/

E 🎧 **12.5 Listen to the recording and complete the conversations.**

1 **A:** Have you ever _worked_ under pressure?   **B:** Yes, I have.

2 **A:** Have you .... for another job?   **B:** No, I haven't.

3 **A:** Has he .... jobs frequently?   **B:** No, he hasn't.

4 **A:** Have they .... the post in newspapers?   **B:** Yes, they have.

5 **A:** Has she .... in marketing before?   **B:** Yes, she has.

6 **A:** Have they .... any training in direct sales?   **B:** No, they haven't.

🎧 **12.5 Listen again and practise saying the sentences.**

Sound work

A job interview

A Read this extract from a job interview. Complete it with items from the box.

> a) Are there any questions you'd like to ask us?
> b) ~~First of all, why do you want this job?~~
> c) I don't think conflict is a bad thing.
> d) In addition, I'm very motivated and ready for a challenge.
> e) Then, I always communicate those aims to the team members.
> f) What are your strengths as a team leader?
> g) What sort of people do you work well with?

A: Well, let's start, then. ...*b*...1

B: I think my excellent experience of project management can contribute to the success of the department. 2

A: You've just mentioned project management. There are twelve people in the project team. 3

B: I like to have clear aims to begin with. I think that's essential for a team leader. ....4 They all need to know exactly where they're going.

A: Right. And what do you do about conflict in a team?

B: There's always some conflict in teams. ....5 You have to listen to people and help them to solve problems together. I think I'm good at that.

A: 6

B: Well, I like to work with motivated and reliable people. And I like people with a sense of humour – that's great.

A: 7

B: I've read your company brochure, but I would like some details of the projects you've been involved in recently...

Listening practice

B 🎧 12.6 **Listen and tick the most appropriate response a), b) or c).**

1 a) Nothing. I enjoyed all of it.
  b) Yes, of course. Things like working to tight deadlines. ✔
  c) Well, I was Assistant Office Manager.

2 a) I saw the advertisement in *The Norwich Herald*.
  b) I've worked for Alfitel for three months, and I'm really enjoying it.
  c) I think I have the right qualifications and experience, and I need a challenge.

3 a) I didn't have an opportunity to use my leadership skills.
  b) No, I didn't. It was a very boring place.
  c) I'd like to be project manager.

4 a) Cycling. Playing chess. And I love classical music.
  b) Well, I don't like paper work.
  c) I'm a good team worker, and I work well under pressure.

5 a) I think people can learn a lot from each other.
  b) I can work one weekend every month.
  c) Yes. I have negotiated contracts with important clients.

6 a) Yes, you can contact me any day after 2:30.
  b) I have included their details in my CV.
  c) Yes, of course. I have informed both of them.

Answer key

Language work

1 Introductions

Vocabulary

A

2 Russia   4 Poland   6 Argentina
3 Sweden   5 Germany

B

2 Japanese   4 Spanish   6 Greek
3 French   5 English

C

Across	Down
6 Sweden	1 Brazil
8 US	2 India
9 Japan	3 Swiss
11 Korean	4 Finnish
	5 Germany
	7 France
	10 UK

D

2 Holland (the Netherlands)   5 Turkey
3 Pakistan   6 Senegal
4 the Czech Republic

E

2 Portuguese   4 Taiwanese   6 Thai
3 Swiss   5 Slovak

F

Group 1	
Adjectives ending in -an	
Country	**Nationality**
Brazil	Brazil**ian**
Germany	Germ**an**
Iran	Iran**ian**
Chile	Chile**an**

Group 2	
Adjectives ending in -ish	
Country	**Nationality**
Poland	Pol**ish**
Spain	Span**ish**
Scotland	Scott**ish**
Finland	Finn**ish**

Group 3	
Adjectives ending in -ese	
Country	**Nationality**
Japan	Japan**ese**
China	Chin**ese**
Sudan	Sudan**ese**
Vietnam	Vietnam**ese**

Group 4	
Adjectives ending in -i	
Country	**Nationality**
Kuwait	Kuwait**i**
Oman	Oman**i**
Bahrain	Bahrain**i**
Iraq	Iraq**i**

Language review

A

2 's (is)   4 's (is)   6 'm (am) / 's (is)
3 are   5 Are   7 are / is

B

2 Where <u>are</u> they from?
3 What'<u>s</u> (What is) her name?
4 My office <u>is</u> in Paris, but I'<u>m</u> (I am) not French.
5 Mrs Lopez <u>is</u> a lawyer.
6 Alex and Rob <u>are</u> from Italy.

C

2 Are Isabel and Luis from Spain?
3 Are you a programmer?
4 Are you and Tom in Marketing?
5 Am I in Room 16 tomorrow?

D

2 a   3 b   4 d   5 c

E

2 Yes, I am.   5 No, she isn't.   7 No, I'm not.
3 No, you aren't.   6 Yes, he is.   8 No, we aren't.
4 Yes, you are.

Writing

A

1 Is your wife <u>a</u> manager?
2 She <u>is</u> married with two children.
3 Tom and Ana <u>are</u> interested in travel.
4 <u>Is</u> Olympic Airways Greek?
5 My boss's favourite sport is <u>football</u>.
6 The sales manager <u>is</u> very busy today.
7 My best friend is Brazilian. He is <u>from</u> Porto Seguro.

B

2 Akemi's   4 What's   6 aren't. / We're
3 company's   5 It's / isn't

C

2 <u>M</u>rs <u>K</u>imura is <u>J</u>apanese.
3 <u>I</u>s <u>N</u>okia <u>D</u>anish?
4 <u>P</u>aul is married with two children.
5 <u>T</u>his is <u>G</u>eorge <u>E</u>llis, from <u>M</u>arketing.
(NB: names of departments are sometimes spelt without a capital, e.g., marketing, accounts, etc.)
6 <u>M</u>r <u>B</u>rown's new boss is from <u>L</u>ondon, <u>O</u>ntario.

D

2 is from Altheim   5 business is
3 a sales manager   6 do business
4 company sells

2 Work and leisure

Vocabulary

A

2 flexible hours
3 travel opportunities
4 expense account
5 sports facilities
6 company cars
7 parking facilities
8 job security

B

2 March
3 winter
4 February
5 Tuesday
6 autumn

C

| 2 in | 4 in | 6 in | 8 on | 10 in |
| 3 on | 5 at | 7 at | 9 on | 11 at |

D

2 on TV
3 the cinema
4 listening to
5 plays tennis
6 on holiday

E

| 2 at | 4 at | 6 in | 8 in | 10 at |
| 3 Ø | 5 Ø | 7 Ø | 9 in | |

Discover the rule

We do **not** use *at* / *in* / *on* before *next*, *this*, *every* or *last* in a time phrase.

F

2 e 3 b 4 a 5 c 6 d 7 c 8 a 9 e 10 b

Language review

A

2 has
3 like
4 goes
5 arrives
6 check
7 has
8 works
9 spends
10 enjoy

B

2 In the evening we usually watch TV.
3 Tony works late two days a week.
4 How often do you visit clients?
5 I often have lunch with colleagues.
6 They are rarely at home on Saturdays.

C

2 a 3 d 4 b 5 g 6 e 7 h 8 c

Writing

A

2 arrives
3 starts
4 discusses
5 has
6 enjoys
7 studies

B

2 She goes to the UK every year in March.
3 Paul sometimes reads the *Financial Times*.
4 They live in Amsterdam, but they aren't Dutch.
5 Their office is in Oxford Street.
6 As you know, I work for the European Commission.
7 The Polish representatives arrive at Heathrow at 7:30 a.m.
8 Louise and Bill are from the United States.
9 How often do you watch the BBC?

C

First name:	*Raoul*
Surname:	*Gautier*
Age:	*24*
Marital status:	Single / ~~Married~~
Occupation:	*PR Manager*
Address:	*47, Avenue Aristide Briand, Toulouse*
Telephone number:	*55 78 43 00*

D

2 e 3 d 4 a 5 c

3 Problems

Vocabulary

A

2 missing 3 lost 4 broken 5 late

B

2 d 3 f 4 e 5 a 6 g 7 c

C

2 ✓
3 ✓
4 Come to our country! The food is delicious and the people are very friendly.
5 My boss is great, and my colleagues are very nice.
6 I can't do it fast enough. I need some help.

D

2 j 3 b 4 e 5 a 6 d 7 i 8 g 9 h 10 c

E

2 c 3 c 4 a 5 b 6 b 7 a

Language review

A

3 She doesn't finish work late. / She finishes work early.
4 We often work at the weekend.
5 They don't sell office equipment.
6 I don't make a lot of phone calls.
7 He writes reports.

B

2 Jim doesn't get lots of e-mails.
3 Jim has regular breaks.
4 Kate and Ross attend a lot of meetings.
5 Kate and Ross don't often entertain foreign visitors.
6 Jim doesn't read the *Financial Times*.

C

2 Kate and Ross get lots of e-mails, but Jim doesn't.
3 Kate and Ross don't have regular breaks, but Jim does.
4 Jim doesn't attend a lot of meetings, but Kate and Ross do.
5 Jim often entertains foreign visitors, but Kate and Ross don't.
6 Kate and Ross read the *Financial Times*, but Jim doesn't.

D

2 any	5 any	8 some
3 a	6 any	9 any
4 a	7 any	10 some

Writing

A

2 Their company has got a cash flow problem.
3 Our order is delayed.
4 It does not work properly.
5 It is very efficient.
6 She has not got an assistant.

B

2 They pay a lot of rent for a small office in the city centre.
3 When does the meeting finish?
4 Bill has got a large office, but he has not got a company car.
5 How many people do they employ?

C

2 She is always on time, and she is very efficient.
3 The new machine is small, but it is very heavy.
4 The report is very long, but it is very easy to understand.
5 There are a lot of changes, and staff are worried about their jobs.
6 Our office is small, but it is in the city centre.

D

2 inform	4 damaged	6 send
3 problem	5 missing	

E

1 The office is small and crowded. In addition, the air conditioning does not work.
2 The screen is small and the picture is not very good. In addition, there is no remote control.
3 The photocopier does not work and there is only one phone line. In addition, the receptionist is never on time.

4 Travel

Vocabulary

A

Across	Down
5 security	2 gate
6 packing	3 duty
9 arrives	4 single
12 leave	7 alarm
	8 fasten
	10 row
	11 seat

B

2 your luggage   3 to queue   4 a platform

C

2 on	5 at / at	8 for
3 by	6 from / to	9 to / to
4 off / to	7 at	10 from / to

D

2 a   3 e   4 b   5 d

E

2 get off / get on	4 arrive
3 miss	5 are delayed

Language review

A

can (ability)	can (permission)	can (what is possible)
2	4	1
3	6	5
7	8	9

B

c 5   d 6   e 8   f 4   g 7   h 2   i 3

C

2 There's (There is)
3 There aren't (There are not)
4 there's (there is)
5 There're (There are)
6 Is there
7 There aren't (There are not)
8 Is there
9 there're (there are)
10 there isn't (there is not)

D

2 there / It	5 There / it
3 It / There	6 it / it / there
4 It / it	

Writing

A

1 Do you want a single or a double room?
2 I'd like to book a room from Sunday 5th to Thursday 9th of this month.
3 I'm ringing to confirm my flight details.
4 Would you like an aisle or a window seat?
5 Can we meet at the railway station at 8:30?
6 There are two restaurants where you can entertain business guests.

B

2 bath	7 cost
3 Please	8 confirm
4 Thank	9 look
5 inform	10 sincerely
6 available	

5 Food and entertaining

Vocabulary

A

2 a **3** c **4** b **5** c **6** a **7** a **8** b **9** c **10** a **11** b

B

Across	Down
4 cod	**1** soup
6 spaghetti	**3** meat
7 lamb	**5** pizza
9 fruit	**6** salad
	8 beef

C

2 c **3** d **4** b **5** a **6** e

D

2 soup **3** salad **4** a receipt **5** a bill

Language review

A

Countable	Uncountable
1 restaurant	**5** beef
2 credit card	**6** fish [1]
3 hamburger	**7** money
4 waiter	**8** soup [2]

[1] *Fish* is uncountable when it means 'a kind of food'; it is countable when it means 'an animal that lives in water'.
[2] *Soup* is usually uncountable: 'We eat a lot of soup in winter'. Sometimes, it can be countable, as in 'They sell a wide range of tinned soups.'

B

singular countable noun	plural countable noun	uncountable noun
+ I'd like a dessert.	+ I'd like some chips.	+ I'd like some soup.
– I don't want a large glass.	– There aren't any tables free.	– We haven't got any milk.
? Is there a Chinese restaurant in town?	? Are there any green apples?	? Is there any meat in it?

C

2 many **6** much
3 much **7** much
4 many **8** many
5 much

D

2 d **3** b **4** a **5** c **6** f **7** e

Writing

A

2 minutes *not* minute
3 it *not* he
4 the *not* a
5 dishes *not* dish
6 meat *not* meet
7 book *not* booking

B

a 2 **b** 1 **c** 5 **d** 6 **e** 4 **f** 3

C

2 book **5** confirm
3 menu **6** again
4 vegetarian **7** Yours

6 Sales

Vocabulary

A

2 a **3** b **4** b **5** c **6** a **7** a

B

Across	Down
4 receipt	**1** period
7 free	**3** return
9 reward	**5** choose
10 benefits	**6** credit
	8 save

C

2 to fax **4** to promote
3 to pay **5** to say

D

2 e **3** f **4** d **5** a **6** c

E

2 retail **5** wholesale
3 competitor **6** after-sales service
4 guarantee period

Language review

A

2 were **6** was / were
3 were **7** were
4 was **8** were
5 were / were / was

B

2 cost **7** sell
3 flew **8** spent
4 got **9** take
5 give **10** wrote
6 paid

C

2 wrote / sent **5** paid
3 got **6** flew
4 spent

D

2 introduced **9** delayed
3 went **10** launched
4 reached **11** went
5 stayed **12** was
6 continued **13** grew
7 increased **14** reached
8 wanted

E

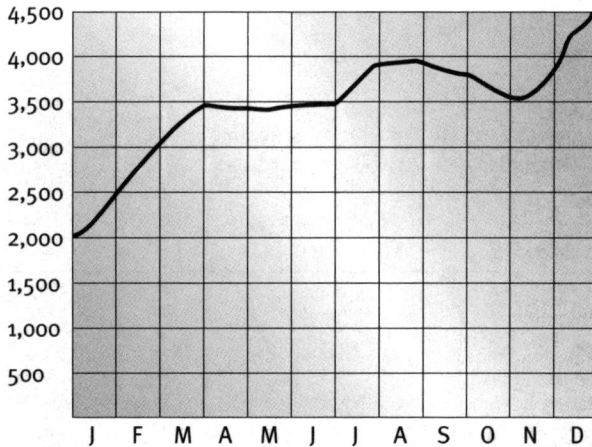

Writing

A

2 Before they place an order, a lot of people like to <u>ask</u> questions.
3 Please quote us <u>a</u> price for the goods listed below.
4 This special promotion is only <u>for</u> a short time.
5 Unfortunately, we wrote the wrong delivery <u>address</u> on the package.
6 We paid a €200 <u>deposit</u> and the rest in 12 monthly instalments.

B

2 launched *not* launch
3 sales *not* sale
4 experienced *not* experience
5 show *not* showing
6 They *not* The

C

The order is: 1, 6, 3, 8, 4, 2, 7, 5

7 People

Vocabulary

A

2 sociable   4 punctual   6 hard-working
3 creative   5 ambitious

B

2 to   5 at   8 on
3 for   6 for   9 with
4 Ø   7 with   10 Ø

C

2 d 3 e 4 a 5 f 6 c

D

un-	in-	im-
unenthusiastic	indecisive	impolite
unreliable	inefficient	impatient
unsociable		

Language review

A

1 began   6 found
2 bring   7 went
3 caught   8 knew
4 came   9 leave
5 drive   10 sent

B

2 drive / caught   7 come (*or* go)
3 leave   8 find
4 send / bring   9 catch
5 begin   10 go
6 knew

C

b 4 c 10 d 8 e 9 f 5 g 1 h 3 i 7 j 2

D

2 Did he like to work in a team?
3 Were they hard-working?
4 Was Mrs Whitehead popular with her colleagues?
5 Did she know how to motivate people?
6 Were you happy to work with Sandra?

E

b 4 c 5 d 2 e 6 f 3

F

2 No, we didn't.   6 Yes, it was.
3 Yes, they did.   7 Yes, they were.
4 No, they weren't.   8 Yes, I can.
5 No, she doesn't.

G

Sample questions
2 Where did her parents move to?
3 Was she a successful student? / Was she born in Aarhus? / Was she good with numbers?
4 What were her favourite subjects?
5 Where did her father work?
6 Did the students like her book?
7 Where did she do an MBA?
8 What did she do at the age of 25?
9 Is Nielsen Electronics successful?
10 How many branches does it have?

Writing

A

2 so   5 because
3 but   6 so
4 because   7 but / because

B

3 is   5 ✔   7 a
4 the   6 any   8 of

C

2 g 3 a 4 d 5 e 6 c 7 b

8 Markets

Vocabulary

A

2 attractive **4** declining **6** mass **8** luxury
3 home **5** mature **7** big **9** niche

Hidden word: *profitable*

B

2 a **3** c **4** b **5** a **6** b **7** c

Language review

A

2 larger **5** younger **8** happier
3 easier **6** newer **9** earlier
4 hotter **7** bigger **10** quieter

B

2 c **3** a **4** d **5** e **6** b

C

2 more **5** younger **8** a
3 difficult **6** most **9** easier
4 the **7** than **10** worse

D

2 a **3** g **4** b **5** f **6** d **7** c

E

Sample answers
2 a little (*or* a bit)
3 a little (*or* a bit) bigger
4 many (*or* a lot) fewer
5 much (*or* a lot) more expensive than
6 is much (*or* a lot) lighter than

Writing

A

2 interested in **4** like to know
3 please confirm **5** look forward to

B

b 5 **c** 3 **d** 2 **e** 4 **f** 1 **g** 7

C

Sample answer

Hi Tom,

Mr Stankov from Impex contacted me this morning. He is very unhappy because he hasn't received the samples of our new products. He says he may not order from us again.

Could you please send him another box of samples as soon as possible. You know Russia is a very important market for us and we don't want to lose this customer.

Many thanks for dealing with this.

Best regards,

Kim

9 Companies

Vocabulary

A

2 manufactures **4** has **6** launched
3 provided **5** exports

B

2 c **3** d **4** e **5** a

C

2 supplied **4** sell abroad
3 employs **5** introduced

D

2 d **3** b **4** f **5** c **6** a

Language review

B

2 listening **5** taking **8** working
3 increasing **6** running **9** trying
4 developing **7** referring **10** dealing

C

2 Many foreign companies <u>are</u> investing in Turkey.
3 <u>Are</u> Sonara's sales figures improving?
4 I'<u>m</u> (I <u>am</u>) looking for a manager with a lot of experience in finance.
5 <u>Is</u> Tom still checking the company accounts?
6 Unfortunately, the east of the country <u>is</u> not attracting many investors.
7 You'<u>re</u> (You <u>are</u>) planning to break into the Spanish market, aren't you?

D

2 Yes, they are. **6** No, I'm not.
3 No, they aren't. **7** Yes, she is.
4 No, he isn't. **8** No, it isn't.
5 Yes, we are.

E

2 are improving / improve **5** test / 's (is) testing
3 takes / is taking **6** 're (are) using / use
4 organises / 's (is) organising

F

2 is answering **7** are thinking
3 does / employ **8** answer
4 is speaking **9** translate
5 are employing **10** speak
6 thinks

Writing

A

3 he *not* she **7** ✓
4 plans *not* plan **8** brands *not* brand
5 make *not* made **9** it also *not* its also
6 wear *not* wearing **10** stores *not* store

B

> Dear Sir or Madam
>
> We are writing to request further information about your new range of trainers.
>
> We are a large chain of retailers of sportswear. We are looking for a manufacturer of footwear for the French market.
>
> We operate from over 400 stores and always order in large quantities. Could you please send us details of special discounts for such orders and your latest catalogue.
>
> We look forward to hearing from you.
>
> Yours faithfully
>
> Barbara Costa

C

2 but also	4 The first one	6 as well as
3 For example	5 The second one	7 Finally

10 The Web

Vocabulary

A

Across		Down	
2 dot	8 e-mail	1 shows	5 fulfils
4 online	9 key	2 debits	6 verify
7 credits		3 website	7 click

B

2 crash   3 search engine   4 download   5 virus

C

2 at	7 to	12 till (until)
3 at	8 out	13 to
4 to	9 for	14 for
5 in	10 on	15 in
6 From	11 in	16 by

Language review

A

2 I'm going to put	5 isn't going to meet
3 're going to expand	6 She's going to call
4 Is (he) going to talk	

B

2 e   3 f   4 a   5 d   6 b

C

2 won't	5 won't	8 will
3 'll	6 won't	9 'll
4 will	7 won't	10 will

D

2 'My computer's not working properly.' 'Don't worry. I'll (or I will) call our IT specialist.'

3 Our visitors from Korea are arriving next Thursday at 11.30.

4 We can't be sure that people will have more free time in 20 years' time.

5 Are you going to apply for the post of Systems Analyst with Crawley Electronics?

6 Do you think you'll (or you will) be able to come to the conference?

7 I can't make it tomorrow morning, I'm afraid. I'm (or I am) giving a talk at the trade fair.

8 It'll (or It will) cost too much to employ an extra IT assistant.

9 We are certain Internet security is going to get better.

10 I'll have the report on your desk before Friday. I promise.

Writing

A

2 He won't catch the earlier flight.

3 He won't check in until 8:45.

4 He hopes there won't be a delay.

5 Judith will book him on a later flight.

6 She won't book him on the early morning flight.

7 Dave arrives at 10:50, so he won't be late for the meeting.

B

2 d   3 e   4 f   5 c   6 a

C

2 leaving	5 later	8 arriving
3 I should	6 Sorry	9 delay
4 Please	7 early	10 you'll

D

Sample answer

> Hi Judith,
>
> TX for looking into this.
>
> PLS book me on the 9:45 flight if that's no problem.
>
> Those flights are usually on time, and they always arrange for someone to pick me up at the airport, so I should be fine.
>
> TX again.
>
> Best,
>
> Dave

11 Cultures

Vocabulary

A

2 a   3 c   4 b   5 a   6 b   7 c   8 c   9 b

B

1 logical	3 natural	5 historical
2 mathematical	4 historic	

C

2 political	5 cultural	7 politics
3 economic	6 economy	8 economical
4 natural		

Language review

A

2 c **3** b **4** f **5** a **6** e

B

2 shouldn't
3 shouldn't
4 should
5 should

6 shouldn't
7 should
8 should

C

2 should
3 shouldn't
4 should
5 should

6 shouldn't
7 shouldn't
8 should
9 shouldn't

D

2 Would you
3 Would you
4 Could I

5 Could you
6 A: Could you / B: Would you

Writing

A

2 but
3 because
4 so

5 but
6 because
7 so

8 and

B

Sample answer

> Dear Ms Roberts,
>
> I enjoy working in Accounts. My colleagues are great and the work is often challenging.
>
> Unfortunately, I have problems with some of the recent changes. I would like my hours of work to be more flexible because of my family situation.
>
> I also have to spend too much time writing reports.
>
> Finally, in the past there was much more face-to-face communication in the company, and that was very good.
>
> I would like to see you to talk about all this in more detail. Could you please let me know when is a good day for you?
>
> Best wishes,
>
> Marco Albu

C

2 c **3** d **4** e **5** a

D

b 3 **c** 5 **d** 1 **e** 4

12 Jobs

Vocabulary

A

2 a **3** c **4** b **5** b **6** a **7** b **8** c **9** b **10** c **11** b

B

2 in
3 in/for

4 in
5 for

6 for
7 as

Language review

A

2 <u>Have</u> Pierre and Lucien <u>changed</u> jobs frequently?
3 <u>Has</u> Anna <u>had</u> several jobs since leaving university?
4 <u>Have</u> Laura and Stella both <u>applied</u> for the same job?
5 <u>Have</u> you and Tim ever <u>had</u> difficulties getting along with Mr Dumas?
6 <u>Have</u> you ever <u>worked</u> in Central Asia?

B

b 1 **c** 6 **d** 3 **e** 4 **f** 5

C

2 they have
3 I (we) have
4 they haven't

5 I (we) haven't
6 has / haven't

D

a 1, 4, 5, 6, 9, 10   **b** 2, 3, 7, 8

E

2 've received (have received)
3 phoned
4 have you selected
5 started
6 arrived
7 haven't finished

8 've already selected (have already selected)
9 Have you invited
10 thought
11 've finished (have finished)
12 didn't have

Writing

A

2 What are your strengths?
3 What do you do in your free time?
4 What kind of people do you work well with?
5 What has been your greatest achievement?
6 What did you like about your last job?
7 What do you want to do in the future?

B

Sample answers

1 I speak German and Italian, and I'm learning Japanese.
2 I'm a very organised person. And I get on well with people.
3 I go swimming every weekend, and I sometimes play tennis.
4 I like to work with reliable people, and I also like people who have a sense of humour.
5 I did really well on my MBA course, and I'm quite proud of that.
6 My colleagues were very helpful, and the atmosphere in our department was great.
7 I expect my job to give me fresh challenges because I want to keep learning and to give the best of myself.

C

2 a **3** e **4** g **5** b **6** f **7** c

Introduction

Vowels

/ɒ/	/e/	/ɑː/
1 job	1 sell	1 card
2 knowledge	2 friendship	2 heart
3 want	3 said	3 laugh

/ eɪ/	/eə/	/aɪ/
1 pay	1 share	1 price
2 break	2 chair	2 buyer
3 train	3 their	3 height

Consonants

/ʃ/	/s/	/j/
1 option	1 sell	1 year
2 conscious	2 advice	2 Europe
3 insurance	3 scientific	3 million

1 Introductions

Sound work

A

3✔ 4✔ 5✘ 6✔ 7✔

D *See audio script 1.4.*

F *See audio script 1.6.*

Survival business English

A

2 f 3 a 4 h 5 g 6 i 7 d 8 j 9 e 10 b

B *See audio script 1.7.*

C

2 a 3 b 4 c 5 a 6 b 7 c 8 a

2 Work and leisure

Sound work

B

2 discusses 3
3 starts 1
4 closes 2
5 delivers 3
6 visits 2
7 changes 2
8 completes 2

C *See audio script 2.3.*

E *See audio script 2.5.*

Survival business English

A 2 f 3 b 4 a 5 d 6 e

B 2 b 3 b 4 c 5 a 6 c 7 a 8 b 9 a 10 c

3 Problems

Sound work

B

/eɪ/ as in *play safe*	/ɒ/ as in *top job*	/æ/ as in *bad bank*	/ɑː/ as in *smart card*
1 dangerous	4 quality	7 travel	10 hard
2 space	5 watch	8 bag	11 part
3 delayed	6 soft	9 narrow	12 fast

C /ɪ/ as in *quick fix.*

E *See audio script 3.5.*

G

Do you work in August?
Do you socialise with colleagues?
Do you like your job?

Survival business English

A and **B**

1 We'll have to walk, I'm afraid. The **lift** is out of order.
2 I can't do the photocopying. We've run out of A4 **paper**. Where can I get some?
3 The coffee **machine** is broken. Let's get a new one.
4 I think there's something wrong with their **phone**. The line is engaged all the time.
5 The **printer** isn't working properly. The paper jams every time I use it.
6 There's a **coffee** stain on this envelope. Can I have another one, please?

C *See audio script 3.9.*

D 2 c 3 b 4 c 5 a 6 c

4 Travel

Sound work

B and **C**

/ə/ as in *about Canada*	/əʊ/ as in *go slow*	/ɒ/ as in *top job*	/ɔː/ as in *short course*	/ʌ/ as in *much luck*
collect	home	office	airport	money
confirm	hotel	shop	passport	come

D 3 − 4 + 5 − 6 + 7 + 8 −

E *See audio script 4.4.*

Survival business English

(A) *See audio script 4.5.*

(B) *See audio script 4.6.*

(C) **2** a **3** c **4** c **5** a **6** b **7** b **8** b **9** a **10** c

5 Food and entertaining

Sound work

(B) *See audio script 5.2.*

(C) *See audio script 5.3.*

(D) *See audio script 5.4.*

Survival business English

(A) *See audio script 5.5.*

(B) **a** 3 **b** 7 **c** 4 **d** 6 **e** 2 **f** 1 **g** 8 **h** 5

(C) **2** b **3** a **4** b **5** c **6** a

6 Sales

Sound work

(A) **2** d **3** e **4** a **5** b **6** g **7** f

(B) *See audio script 6.2.*

(C) *See audio script 6.3.*

Survival business English

(A) *See audio script 6.4.*

(B) **2** a **3** b **4** c **5** b **6** c **7** a **8** c

7 People

Sound work

(A) *See audio script 7.1.*

(C) *See audio script 7.3.*

(D) *See audio script 7.4.*

Survival business English

(A)

2 too
3 down
4 manage
5 suggestion
6 leave

(B)
b 1 **c** 2 **d** 5 **e** 6 **f** 3

(C)

Speaker 1: b
Speaker 2: d
Speaker 3: c
Speaker 4: b
Speaker 5: a
Speaker 6: d
Speaker 7: a
Speaker 8: c

(D)

2 a **3** c **4** b **5** b **6** a

8 Markets

Sound work

(C) *See audio script 8.3.*

(D)

2 aTTRACtive (but: MARketing; COMpany)
3 QUAlity (but: dePARTment; proDUcer)
4 comPEtitive (but: PROfitable; COMfortable)
5 perCENT (but: THOUsand; MILlion)
6 MARket (but: maTURE; sucCESS)

Survival business English

(A) *See audio script 8.5.*

(B)

b Agreeing: 1, 4
c Disagreeing: 2
d Making a suggestion: 5

(C)

a 5 **b** 3 **c** 6 **d** 1 **e** 2 **f** 4

(D)

2 a **3** a **4** c **5** b **6** b

9 Companies

Sound work

(A) *See audio script 9.1.*

(C) *See audio script 9.3.*

(E) *See audio script 9.5.*

Survival business English

(A)

2 c   3 f   4 e   5 b   6 a

(B)

Greeting the audience: 3 and 4
Introducing the topic: 1 and 6
Giving a plan of the talk: 2 and 5

(C)

1 b   2 b   3 c   4 b   5 a

10 The Web

Sound work

(B) See audio script 10.2.

(C) See audio script 10.3.

(F) See audio script 10.6.

Survival business English

(A)

Speaker 2: a
Speaker 3: b
Speaker 4: e
Speaker 5: d
Speaker 6: c
Speaker 7: e
Speaker 8: c
Speaker 9: d
Speaker 10: a

(B)

2 a   3 b   4 c   5 b   6 a

11 Cultures

Sound work

(A) See audio script 11.1.

(B) See audio script 11.2.

(C)

O o custom /ə/	o O abroad /ə/	O o o cultural /ə/ /ə/	o O o appointment /ə/ /ə/
silence offer	arrive adapt	popular document	important arrangement

(E)

3 ✔   4 ✘   5 ✔   6 ✘

Survival business English

(A) See audio script 11.6

(B) 2 c   3 b   4 b   5 c   6 a

12 Jobs

Sound work

(B) See audio script 12.2.

(C) See audio script 12.3.

(E) See audio script 12.5.

Survival business English

(A) 2 d   3 f   4 e   5 c   6 g   7 a

(B) 2 c   3 a   4 c   5 a   6 c

Audio scripts

Introduction

The sounds of English

Vowel sounds

/ɪ/	quick fix	/ɔː/	short course	
/iː/	clean sheet	/ʊ/	good books	
/e/	sell well	/uː/	school rules	
/æ/	bad bank	/ʌ/	much luck	
/ɑː/	smart card	/ɜː/	first term	
/ɒ/	top job	/ə/	a'bout 'Canada	

Diphthongs

/eɪ/	play safe	/əʊ/	go slow
/aɪ/	my price	/ɪə/	near here
/ɔɪ/	choice oil	/eə/	fair share
/aʊ/	downtown	/ʊə/	tour

Consonants

1 Contrasting voiceless and voiced consonants

Voiceless		Voiced	
/p/	pay	/b/	buy
/f/	file	/v/	value
/t/	tax	/d/	deal
/θ/	think	/ð/	this
/tʃ/	cheap	/dʒ/	job
/s/	sell	/z/	zero
/k/	card	/g/	gain
/ʃ/	option	/ʒ/	decision

2 Other consonants

/m/	mine	/l/	loss	/n/	net	/r/	rise
/ŋ/	branding	/w/	win	/h/	high	/j/	year

1 Introductions

1.1
1 German; Turkish
2 France; Japan
3 Poland; Oman
4 Swedish; Greek
5 Russian; Kuwaiti
6 England; Italy
7 Brazilian; American

1.2
France; French
Spain; Spanish
Denmark; Danish
Wales; Welsh

1.3
an engineer; She's an engineer.
a sales assistant; He's a sales assistant in a supermarket.

1.4
1 Peter is an accountant in Aachen.
2 Azim is an Uzbek airline pilot.
3 This is Olga. She works in Omsk.
4 Tim, meet Alan. He's in Accounts.
5 Liz works as a chemist for an Irish company.

1.5
Bra.zil; Bra.zil.ian
Chi.na; Chi.nese

1.6
1 She's from A.mer.i.ca; She's A.mer.i.can
2 He's from It.al.y; He's I.tal.ian
3 They're from Brit.ain; They're Brit.ish
4 I'm from Ja.pan; I'm Jap.a.nese
5 We're from Can.a.da; We're Ca.na.di.an
6 It's from Pol.and; It's Pol.ish
7 So you're from Hun.gar.y; So you're Hun.gar.i.an

1.7
A: Hello. My name's Francis – Francis Wells. I'm the new accountant.
B: Hi! I'm Tom Murphy. Nice to meet you, Francis.
A: Pleased to meet you, Tom. Are you in Accounts, too?
B: No, I'm not. I'm in Sales. I'm Assistant Sales Manager.
A: Mm, that's interesting. And how's business?
B: Not too bad, not too bad.

1.8
1 Is he an accountant?
2 Are you with Nokia?
3 Are you French?
4 Are you married?
5 Is she the new sales assistant?
6 Are they all from Japan?
7 Would you like a coffee?
8 Is Kauf a German company?

2 Work and leisure

2.1
likes; works;
opens; watches;
telephones; finishes

2.2
travels; discusses; starts; closes; delivers; visits; changes; completes

2.3
/ɪ/ as in quick fix
winter; office; Swiss; dinner

/aɪ/ as in my price
Friday; night; client; design; cycling; arrive

2.4

a large_office; in_a large_office; He works_in_a large_office

2.5

1 He works_until_8_o'clock.
2 He's_interested_in_advertising.
3 She gets_up_at 6_and does_exercises.
4 She does_a lot_of_overtime.
5 He has_a lot_of meetings_in the afternoon.

2.6

1 a) A magazine, sometimes.
   b) No, but I write a lot of letters.
   c) About once a month.
2 a) Well, I usually arrive at 8:30.
   b) I go to Geneva twice a year.
   c) Yes, I work a lot every day.
3 a) I usually arrive early.
   b) Around 4:30.
   c) Sometimes, in summer.
4 a) Yes, but I don't like answering the phone.
   b) In the morning. It's very quiet.
   c) My colleagues. They're just fantastic!
5 a) It's really good at the moment.
   b) With Japan, sometimes with Russia.
   c) Twenty thousand euros.
6 a) I think it's one of the Baltic states.
   b) No, I work for Siemens.
   c) No, but I live and work in Tallinn.
7 a) I'm really keen on football and on jogging.
   b) Yes. Of course I do.
   c) Well, I don't enjoy doing overtime.
8 a) Every day, but not on Fridays.
   b) Thirty-five. But I often do overtime.
   c) Yes. I really enjoy having flexible hours.
9 a) Once a week, on Friday mornings.
   b) Meetings usually start at 9 o'clock.
   c) Well, I always enjoy meeting new people.
10 a) Yes. I want to work for an international company.
   b) I'm always busy on Wednesdays.
   c) Good people to work with. And enough money to live on!

3 Problems

3.1

late; want; carry; can't

3.2

1 dangerous; 2 space; 3 delayed; 4 quality; 5 watch; 6 soft; 7 travel; 8 bag; 9 narrow; 10 hard; 11 part; 12 fast

3.3

manager; package; damaged

3.4

Do you live in a city?
Do you go to meetings?
How often do you travel abroad?
What do you do?

3.5

1 Do you drive to work?
2 What time do you start work?
3 When do you finish work?
4 Who do you report to?
5 Why do you do so much overtime?

3.6

Do you work in an office?
Do you travel a lot?

3.7

Do you work in August?
Do you socialise with colleagues?
Do you like your job?

3.8

1 We'll have to walk, I'm afraid. The lift is out of order.
2 I can't do the photocopying. We've run out of A4 paper. Where can I get some?
3 The coffee machine is broken. Let's get a new one.
4 I think there's something wrong with their phone. The line is engaged all the time.
5 The printer isn't working properly. The paper jams every time I use it.
6 There's a coffee stain on this envelope. Can I have another one, please?

3.9

Belco: Good morning. Belco Electronics. How can I help you?
Steve: Good morning. Steve Jenkins here. Well, it's about the *Max 3000* computer software. I'm afraid there are no instructions in the box.
Belco: Oh, I'm very sorry to hear that. It's the *Max 3000* you bought yesterday, is it?
Steve: Yes, that's right.
Belco: Well, Mr Jenkins, just give me your address, and I'll send you the instructions.
Steve: It's Flat 3, 18 Duke Road.
Belco: Right. I've got that. I'll put an instructions manual in the post for you straight away. And once again, sorry about our mistake.
Steve: Thank you very much. Goodbye.
Belco: Goodbye.

3.10

1 Could I speak to Mr Pinto, please?
2 I'm phoning about the new air conditioner. It doesn't work.
3 I'm afraid my invoice is wrong.
4 You're a bit late this morning.
5 Why don't they come to work on time?
6 Good morning, Sunrise Electronics. Ana Schwarz speaking.

4 Travel

4.1

office; home; money; airport; collect

4.2

/ə/ as in about Canada: collect; confirm
/əʊ/ as in go slow: home; hotel
/ɒ/ as in top job: office; shop
/ɔː/ as in short course: airport; passport
/ʌ/ as in much luck: money; come

4.3

1 You can come.
2 They can't go.
3 He can't drive.
4 We can try.
5 She can't type.
6 I can wait.
7 She can pay.
8 You can't choose.

4.4

1 Can I use the phone, please?
2 Can I have a receipt, please?
3 Can I have the bill, please?
4 Can I have a glass of water, please?
5 Can I take one of these brochures, please?
6 Can I have an alarm call at 6:15, please?

4.5

1 A: So the first name is spelt F-R-A-N-C-I-S.
  B: No. It's F-R-A-N-C-E̱-S.
2 A: And the phone number is 3228 5959.
  B: Sorry, no. It's 3228 58̱5̱9̱.
3 A: Ms Salgado's flight number is IP3208.
  B: Can you check that again, please? The number I have here is IḆ3208.

4.6

1 A: So you need two single rooms for three nights, from the twenty-third of this month?
  B: No. We need them from the twenty-fi̱ṟs̱ṯ.
2 A: Right. One double room with shower for two nights.
  B: Sorry. I'd like one with ba̱ṯẖ, if possible.
3 A: ... and an aisle seat for Ms Sandra Davis. D-A-V-I-S ...
  B: Sorry, no. D-A-V-I-E̱-S
4 A: The train leaves from platform eighteen, is that right?
  B: No sir. You want platform si̱x̱ṯe̱e̱ṉ for Newcastle.
5 A: Is the fitness centre on the ground floor?
  B: No, madam. It's on the fo̱u̱ṟṯẖ floor.
6 A: Let me just write this down ... Two hundred and fifty euros, and ...
  B: Sorry, no. That's two hundred and ṯẖi̱ṟṯy̱ euros.

4.7

1 a) Platform 5.
  b) At 6:30, if it's not delayed.
  c) Yes, and sometimes by plane.
2 a) Of course. You can just sit on the balcony and enjoy the view.
  b) Yes, there's CNN and BBC in each room.
  c) Every room has a computer, sir.
3 a) Yes. All flights are delayed.
  b) It's 020 7864 3400.
  c) Of course. Go ahead.
4 a) You can take a taxi or the airport minibus.
  b) You can make a reservation today.
  c) Only half an hour, by bus.
5 a) Yes. There's a Lufthansa flight at 9:10.
  b) Single or return?
  c) No, I'm afraid you need to change at Toronto.
6 a) Yes. It opens at 7:30.
  b) Yes. How can I help you?
  c) No, but their fitness centre is great.

7 a) Yes, of course. Would you like an aisle or a window seat?
  b) Sure. What's the name of the company, sir?
  c) Yes. That's 35 euros, please.
8 a) It arrives at 15:20.
  b) It's G3 1748.
  c) From gate 26.
9 a) What's your room number?
  b) I'm afraid that's too late.
  c) That's right. From platform 5.
10 a) The 3:30 flight to Qatar is now boarding.
  b) That's row 22, seat F.
  c) From terminal 2.

5 Food and entertaining

5.1

Tim; team
sit; seat

5.2

/ɪ/ as in quick fix: bill; manager; chicken; business
/iː/ as in clean sheet: sweet; meal; receipt; Sweden

5.3

1 It's for you.
2 How about some dessert?
3 Why don't we invite them for dinner?
4 Would you like some more juice?
5 How much time do you have for lunch?
6 There aren't a lot of restaurants in this area.
7 What do you recommend for the main course?
8 They have a lot of fish dishes on the menu.

5.4

service; business; menu
dessert; receipt
company; restaurant
spaghetti; delicious

5.5

1 Do you like Italian food?
2 Shall I ask for a menu in English?
3 Are you ready to order?
4 What would you like for the main course?
5 How's your food?
6 Now, Bob, how about a dessert?
7 Would you like to have coffee or tea?
8 Right. Shall we get the bill?

5.6

D = Dieter; B = Bob

1 D: Do you like Italian food?
   B: Oh yes, I love it.
2 D: Shall I ask for a menu in English?
   B: No, that's all right, thanks. I need to practise my German a bit.
3 D: Are you ready to order?
   B: I think I need a few more minutes.
4 D: What would you like for the main course?
   B: Mm. Some lasagna would be nice.
5 D: How's your food?
   B: Very nice, thank you. We must come here again next time I'm in Frankfurt.
6 D: Now, Bob, how about a dessert?
   B: No, thanks. I don't really like sweet things.
7 D: Would you like to have coffee or tea?
   B: Mm, yeah. I'd love an espresso, actually.
8 D: Right. Shall we get the bill?
   B: Yes, let's. It's getting late.

5.7

1 Is that enough soup for you?
2 More rice?
3 What would you like to drink?
4 Would you like some more salmon?
5 Could you pass the salt, please?
6 Would you like some more?

6 Sales

6.1

1 grew; knew
2 bought; caught
3 gave; paid
4 got; cost
5 said; met
6 sold; wrote
7 took; put

6.2

1 Delivery's free.
2 There was no extra cost.
3 How much are they?
4 It was a great deal.
5 They're at the office.
6 We were away on business.
7 These models are easy to use.
8 The design's interesting.
9 We're looking for experienced sales reps.
10 They were on time.

6.3

1 talked; launched; stopped; worked
2 started; finished; needed; offered
3 increased; advised; improved; received
4 invited; expanded; exported; promoted

6.4

1 The *Tex23* is our most popular laptop computer bag. It's designed for the business traveller, and it's available in black or dark brown leather.
2 *LockIt* is an excellent protection against car crime. It's made of steel and is very strong.
3 With our new *Medico* testing kit, busy executives get useful and reliable information about their health. It's easy to use because it's fully automatic. And it's so small you can carry it in your briefcase.
4 The *Dual EM* mobile phone is in the low price range, but it has a lot of special features. For example, you can read and write e-mail messages anywhere in the world.
5 Made for busy office people, the *Exex* desk chair is stylish and very well designed. *Exex* is the solution to your back problems.
6 With the *Storage Wizard* you can find any of your CDs or CD-ROMs quickly and easily. It's a very practical storage system that saves a lot of space and a lot of time.

6.5

1 Do you give a guarantee?
2 Do you have these goods in stock?
3 Could we pay in instalments?
4 What colours is this model available in?
5 Does it have any special features?
6 How expensive are they?
7 What's the target market?
8 What about delivery?

7 People

7.1

1 spend; spread; spring
2 staff; stress; strong
3 skill; screen; script
4 practical; problem; practise
5 helpful; punctual
6 increase; expand

7.2

an_office; in_an_office; He works_in_an_office.

7.3

1 I met_Edit_in_April.
2 I didn't send_it_out_on time.
3 She got_on well with_others.
4 He had_a lot_of interesting_ideas.
5 It was_a bad_idea to sell_it.

7.4

1 A: Was Philip a good colleague?
   B: Yes, he was.
2 A: Did Barbara leave the company?
   B: No, she didn't.
3 A: Were they experienced?
   B: Yes, they were.
4 A: Did you do a lot of research?
   B: No, we didn't.
5 A: Was it a successful year for the company?
   B: No, it wasn't.
6 A: Did he often work late?
   B: Yes, he did.

7.5

1 How did you get to the office?
2 Where did she start her journey?
3 When did they found the company?
4 How old were they?
5 How far was it?

7.6

Speaker 1:
All right, then. I'll think about it and get back to you by the end of the week.
Speaker 2:
Let me tell you why they are thinking of leaving the company. No job security; unpaid overtime; and only ten days annual leave: that's why!
Speaker 3:
We could, for example, move Marko to a different department.
Speaker 4:
I understand what you're saying, but we can't hire any more staff this year.
Speaker 5:
There's too much work in Admin. Three people are trying to do the work of ten.
Speaker 6:
If so many employees are unhappy, it's partly because we don't have a proper cafeteria, and we don't have any parking facilities whatsoever.
Speaker 7:
We don't offer enough opportunities for promotion. We simply don't think enough about all the brilliant, ambitious employees that we have.
Speaker 8:
Why don't we hire some part-time staff?

7.7

1 a) He never helped anyone.
   b) Yes, it was hard work.
   c) Because I didn't like my colleagues.
2 a) What kind of help do you need?
   b) Sorry, but everybody says I can do a great job.
   c) Thanks. I need a lot of support, too.
3 a) No, but he is very helpful.
   b) The problem is, business is bad.
   c) Well, he's rude sometimes.
4 a) I think there's a meeting.
   b) They just have too much work.
   c) Just a headache. I'll be better tomorrow.
5 a) Yes. My assistant has a lot of work, too.
   b) OK. What about a part-time one?
   c) Fine, but why did he leave the company?
6 a) Right. Let's try and solve this problem together.
   b) Well, they want to get to the top as fast as they can.
   c) I work long hours every day.

8 Markets

8.1

ma.ture   a.ttract.ive   qual.it.y
/ə/   /ə/   /ə/
suc.cess   con.sum.er   hol.i.day
/ə/   /ə/   /ə/   /ə/

8.2

1 better; better than; It's better than last month.
2 cheaper; cheaper than; Life is cheaper here than in Paris.
3 heavier; heavier than; This model is heavier than the RT100.

8.3

1 Our market share is increasing faster here than in Korea.
2 The Hilton is bigger than the Palace.
3 Our main competitor offers a cheaper service than we do.
4 The rate of unemployment is worse than last year's.
5 She's more popular than our manager.

8.4

1 marketing; attractive; company
2 quality; department; producer
3 profitable; competitive; comfortable
4 thousand; million; percent
5 market; mature; success

8.5

1 I think you're right.
2 I'm afraid I don't agree.
3 How do you feel about this?
4 I really like the idea.
5 What about re-launching it in May?

8.6

1 Where should we sell our new product?
2 Now then. What kind of person is our target consumer?
3 Where should we advertise?
4 Why is our new product losing market share?
5 In your opinion, when is a good time to re-launch our product?
6 Should we do some more market research?

9 Companies

9.1

aisle; debt; island; salmon
answer; fasten; know; sandwich
autumn; foreign; lamb; talk
climb; half; receipt; Wednesday

9.2

1 We are looking for a bigger warehouse.
2 Five companies are competing for this contract.
3 Our profit figures are improving.
4 Many German companies are investing in Turkey.

9.3

1 You're opening a subsidiary in Toulouse, is that right?
2 They're setting up joint ventures with Chinese companies.
3 What are they doing research into?
4 Our competitors are expanding abroad.
5 What are we trying to achieve?
6 Where are you looking for new offices?

9.4

1 We <u>aren't</u> looking for new markets.
2 They <u>aren't</u> competing for that contract.
3 Our turnover <u>isn't</u> increasing.
4 She <u>isn't</u> working tomorrow.

9.5

1 <u>They aren't</u> investing in Indonesia.
2 <u>She isn't</u> planning to start a new business.
3 <u>We aren't</u> attracting a lot of new customers.
4 <u>It isn't</u> growing very fast.
5 <u>They aren't</u> launching it until September.

9.6

1 Man: We're looking for new offices.
  Woman: What's wrong with this building? Too small?
  Man: Well, it's big enough, but it's much too expensive.
2 Woman: So, what do you think of February's sales figures, Fred?
  Man: They're certainly much better than last month's.
  Woman: A lot! And they're still going up, you know.
3 Man: Everybody says Tom and Chris are in Azerbaijan to set up a joint venture.
  Woman: That's not quite right. Only Chris is there, and she just wants to negotiate a contract.
  Man: Oh dear. Sometimes people don't know what they're talking about!
4 Woman: First, I'd like to talk about the features of the new product.
  Man: How about starting with the background to the launch?
  Woman: That's a good idea. Then I can present the features just before the marketing plan.
5 Man: Our marketing strategy isn't good. Sales figures are getting worse.
  Woman: Yes they are, but I think our strategy's fine. In my opinion, there's a problem with our product.
  Man: You mean, it's not right for that market?

10 The Web

10.1

video; win
value; way

10.2

1 Their website is very exciting.
2 In my view, it's a waste of money.
3 Which site do you visit most often?
4 The World Wide Web is of great value to advertisers.
5 If you want to visit that site, you need a valid password.
6 I received a virus warning.

10.3

1 We'll take the early flight.
2 They work hard.
3 I'll do it for them.
4 You'll have to download it.
5 They buy the same software.
6 We'll try all the search engines.

10.4

1 **I'll** show you.
2 **You'll** need it.
3 **He'll** want one.
4 **She'll** buy them.
5 **We'll** watch it.
6 **They'll** do it.

10.5

1 A: So the flight's boarding at Gate 30.
  B: No, it's Gate <u>13</u> we want.
2 A: Right. So I can come any Tuesday.
  B: Sorry, no. I said any <u>Thurs</u>day.

10.6

1 A: ... and you said check-in is at nine o'clock.
  B: No, it's <u>eight</u> o'clock, I'm afraid.
2 A: ... so that's Janet G-R-A-Y.
  B: Sorry, no. G-R-<u>E</u>-Y. Mrs Janet Grey.
3 A: Excuse me. Is the presentation on the first floor?
  B: No, it's on the <u>third</u> floor. You'd better take the lift!
4 A: ... and your e-mail address is Vermeulen@pe.org.
  B: That's not quite right. It's <u>B</u>-E, as in Belgium.
5 A: Let me just read the postcode back to you: CM20 3GE.
  B: No. It's CM20 3<u>J</u>E.
6 A: So the fax number of their Sofia office is 359 2 968 61 58.
  B: ... 61 <u>98</u>.

10.7

Speaker 1:
Yes, I can do Thursday afternoon.
Speaker 2:
What's a good time for you?
Speaker 3:
OK. Tomorrow 9 a.m. is fine for me too.
Speaker 4:
I'm terribly sorry I didn't come to your presentation. I was ill.
Speaker 5:
If Monday's too busy, maybe Wednesday, then?
Speaker 6:
Sorry, I can't do Monday morning.
Speaker 7:
I'm sorry I didn't make it on time.
Speaker 8:
I'm afraid I can't make Thursday or Friday.
Speaker 9:
How about Tuesday morning instead?
Speaker 10:
What day suits you?

10.8

1 Man: About the contract. Can we discuss it on Tuesday? Monday's no good.
  Woman: You'll be in Stockholm all day Tuesday, so I suggest the day after, if that's convenient.
  Man: Oh, of course. OK then. Fine.
2 Woman: I'm terribly sorry I forgot there was a staff meeting this morning.
  Man: Don't worry. We just discussed things, but we didn't take any decisions.
  Woman: What a pity! Well, I didn't miss much, it seems.
3 Man: So my flight is tomorrow at 2:45.
  Woman: How will you get to the airport? Will you go by metro, or do you need a taxi?
  Man: I'll just take the company car this time. I'm coming back early on Wednesday.

4 Woman: Sandra is not available right now. Would you like to leave a message?

Man: Yes please. Can she call me back before 11:30?

Woman: Sure. I'll tell her as soon as she comes out of the meeting.

5 Man: Sorry I didn't make it on time. Our airport is really terrible!

Woman: What happened? All flights delayed again because of the weather?

Man: No, no problem with the weather today, but we waited over half an hour for our luggage.

6 Woman: The conference is from 10:00 to 4:00, so I could meet you there before or afterwards.

Man: Let's meet before, say, 9:00 at the registration desk? Or in the cafeteria maybe?

Woman: All right. So we'll try their famous espresso as soon as we get there!

11 Cultures

11.1
1 first; requests; hosts
2 staff; store; strategy
3 speak; space; special
4 starts; stopped; strict
5 sports; spirits; specialists

11.2
1 In Finland, you should never arrive late for an appointment.
2 In many countries, you shouldn't write on business cards.
3 You shouldn't offer your hand to shake immediately.
4 In Germany, you should use the person's title before the surname.
5 In most countries, you shouldn't point your finger at the person you're talking to.
6 So, before you go to a new country, you should do your homework!

11.3
1 custom; silence; offer
2 abroad; arrive; adapt
3 cultural; popular; document
4 appointment; important; arrangement

11.4
1 Could I use your phone?
2 Could I use your computer?
3 Would you like a drink?
4 Would you like a sandwich?
5 Could you tell me the way?
6 Could you check these figures?

11.5
1 Would you like some coffee?
2 Could you spell that for me?
3 Could I use the meeting room?
4 Would you like a copy of the brochure?
5 Could you make the travel arrangements for me?
6 Could I borrow your dictionary?

11.6
A: So you're saying there are problems in Sales. What kind of problems?
B: Well, it's the representatives. They're complaining about our new work schedule.

A: Do you know what the best thing to do is? Explain to them *why* we changed the schedule.
B: I think they understand the reasons. But, unfortunately, they still don't agree with a lot of the changes.
A: Well, maybe you should talk to them one by one. And try to find out exactly what each one of them is unhappy about.
B: OK then. I'll try that.

11.7
1 Is it a good idea to call staff by their first names?
2 What's the problem with Paolo? He's always late and he never comes to meetings.
3 Should I accept a business card with my right hand?
4 So, what are normal working hours in your country?
5 I'd like to find out a few things about the history of Brazil.
6 Do people usually drink tea or coffee?

12 Jobs

12.1
not; nought   spot; sport   top job; short course

12.2
1 How often do you write reports?
2 What sorts of bosses have you had?
3 Our office staff don't wear uniforms.
4 Robert has taught abroad for four years.

12.3
1 She's gained a lot of experience.
2 I've finished everything.
3 He hasn't sent his CV.
4 They've invited her for an interview.
5 We haven't selected anyone.
6 We've interviewed everyone.

12.4
A: Have you ever worked in a bank?
B: Yes, I have.
A: Has she done anything that shows leadership?
B: Yes, I think she has.

12.5
1 A: Have you ever worked under pressure?
   B: Yes, I have.
2 A: Have you applied for another job?
   B: No, I haven't.
3 A: Has he changed jobs frequently?
   B: No, he hasn't.
4 A: Have they advertised the post in newspapers?
   B: Yes, they have.
5 A: Has she worked in marketing before?
   B: Yes, she has.
6 A: Have they had any training in direct sales?
   B: No, they haven't.

12.6
1 Have you learnt anything from your last job?
2 Why are you applying for this job?
3 What didn't you like about your last job?
4 What are your strengths?
5 What do you think of teamwork?
6 Can we contact your referees?